MEMPHIS, 1828

Drawn by Charles Alexandre Lesueur. See Appendix A.

The
Founding of Memphis
1818-1820

cordially,
James Roper

JAMES ROPER
President, The West Tennessee Historical Society

SESQUICENTENNIAL
MEMPHIS
1819-1969

Published Under the Auspices of
THE MEMPHIS SESQUICENTENNIAL, INC.

CONTENTS

Map photographs by Marc Dickey

FOREWORD

The Memphis Sesquicentennial in the midst of its fitting festivities and fanfares has desired to leave behind a permanent contribution to the history of Memphis. In response to its request, this work is an attempt to get together in one place a comprehensive and accurate account of that event for which this year is the one hundred and fiftieth anniversary—the actual founding of Memphis, from the appointment of the commissioners for the Chickasaw Treaty in May, 1818, through the opening of the land office on the Bluff in December, 1820.

Existing data about this two-year period tend to be scattered, inadequate, and often erroneous. The present effort goes back to primary and contemporary sources as much as possible: correspondence, newspapers, public records, and private documents. Reminiscence and yarn have been kept at bay except when they must serve, and then are properly labeled. Only the dullest pedant would hope to kill a good yarn, and only the naivest researcher would expect to, but there are occasions when sorting out fact from fiction is useful (and sometimes history fascinates more than legend, in the end). Much of the information included herein is appearing in the annals of Memphis for the first time and will, I hope, be of interest even to the local buffs.

The nucleus of this book is two articles, one published in the *Delta Review* for February, 1969, the other a paper read before the West Tennessee Historical Society in May, 1969. The co-operation of both editorial staffs is appreciated in permitting use of material. However, since research for these works was done, much new information has turned up. The Manuscript Division of the Tennessee Archives has recently been brought into excellent order, and several letters and other records of 1819-1820 have become accessible where previously they were not. Also, it has been possible this past summer to do research in depth both in Nashville and in the Library of Congress.

As a result, a good deal of information can now be furnished which was not included even in the articles of a few months ago. Among the items of major interest now presented in print for the first time are these:

the exact date of Fort Pickering's founding, and details of its demise;

new facts about the time of arrival and background of the Carr family, the first settlers after the treaty;

the exact date of arrival of Marcus Winchester and William Lawrence to lay out the town, and details of their departure and trip;

A behind-the-scenes look at the maneuvering which produced Shelby County, with Overton's part made clear where formerly it "could not be stated historically";

the more or less precise location of the Indian trails leading south to Fort Pickering and Nonconnah Creek;

the exact location of the first tavern, built by Tom Carr for the land office;

new light on the 1819 map helping to date positively the Archives town plan;

the beginning date and the schedule of the first regular mail service into Memphis;

the existence and the location of the first cotton gin in the Memphis area.

I thank all those who have helped, especially Miss Mary Davant, Mrs. Gladys Roudebush, and their patient staff at the Cossitt-Goodwyn Library, along with Mrs. Cleo A. Hughes, Senior Archivist, and the equally obliging staff of the Manuscripts Division of the State Library and Archives. Thanks also go to the staff of the Burrow Library of Southwestern at

Memphis for intellectual and other sustenance, and particularly to the Memphis Sesquicentennial for making this publication possible.

JAMES ROPER

Southwestern at Memphis
November 15, 1969

PROLOGUE

The Fourth Chickasaw Bluff, 1541-1818

PROLOGUE

The earliest inhabitant of the Memphis area, so far as the record shows, was an accommodating mastodon who struggled through the swamps destined to be the campus of Southwestern at Memphis till he reached the site of the biology department, where his bones would come to light 23,000 years later.

The story of humankind in West Tennessee begins with the paleolithic Indians of at least 8000 years ago and probably long before. About that time various progressive red men around the country were earning the title of Archaic by learning to weave baskets and make weapons and tools by grinding and polishing stone. However, West Tennesseans were among the conservatives, and it took some of them 6000 years to catch up. By that time Archaic really was archaic, and pottery, agriculture, and ceremonial mounds had become the fashion, which they continued to be from about 1000 B.C. to about 500 A.D. These avant-garde tribes are known as the Woodland Indians. Further developments among them brought on cosmopolitan living with improved methods of raising corn and the rise of priests and politicians, until by 800 A.D. there were city states with formalized patterns of living. Some of these sophisticates, known as Mississippians, built up a string of towns along the Mississippi River some 40 miles long.

The most northern of these towns were situated on the bluff which began at the river to be known as Wolf and stretched away southward in a high and broad plain, the most promising dwelling site between the Ohio and Vicksburg. It was the fourth such escarpment, counting downstream from the mouth of the Ohio. It would become known to history as the Fourth Chickasaw Bluff, but its first settlers were not the ancestors of the Chickasaws. Rather, they had affinities with the later Tunica-Natchez tribes.

11

At the extreme north edge of the group of towns was the one which today is commemorated by the mounds in Memphis' De Soto Park. Then came the one on the bluff just south of Nonconnah Creek, which some four hundred years after it passed from history would be named retroactively "Chucalissa," a Choctaw word meaning "house abandoned" which the Mississippians themselves would not have understood. They told De Soto their constellation of towns was called "Quiz Quiz," and one decoding of the term has it mean "panther's rump," leaving the historian to wonder if the Indians had their own way of being flippant with intrusive strangers. In the 16th century they fell under the power of a budding emperor known as Pacaha, whose capital was probably at Osceola, Arkansas.

In northeast Mississippi in the 16th century lived the Chickasaws. These fierce warriors, though comparatively small in number, commanded a healthy respect from their neighbors, especially their nearest kinsmen the Choctaws to the south. The traditions of both tribes agreed that they had been one people long ago west of the Mississippi, and that they had crossed the river in obedience to the direction given by a magic pole which, stuck in the ground at evening, would point in the morning in the way they should go. It may have been, ironically, that they came from the same Oklahoma region to which they were later exiled.

There are three versions of the further details of their journey and separation. One Choctaw legend has it that the united people crossed the river at the Fourth Bluff, at which place a disagreement arose. One faction walked out of the council, thereby becoming the first secessionists of the Bluff and acquiring a new name, "Chickasaws" or "Rebels." Another Choctaw story keeps the people united until they reached the west bank of the Yazoo River and built a great mound, three acres in extent and forty feet high, known as Nunih Wai-ya. After some time had passed a serious disagreement occurred and the separation took place.

The Chickasaw version is that the tribes separated before crossing the Mississippi, and they, the Chickasaws, crossed at the Fourth Bluff and continued eastward till the magic pole stood upright near Tuscumbia, Alabama, at a spot later known as Chickasaw Old Town (in 1818 the treaty ground). After three years here, the whimsical pole leaned eastward once more, and the tribe set out until they reached the Atlantic near Savannah, Georgia. Evidence of their presence there exists. But a fearful plague struck suddenly, the tribe was decimated, and finally the remnant of the frightened people retreated to the Old Town, where the rash pole stood meekly upright till it rotted.

In historical times the Chickasaws had moved a few miles southwest to the headwaters of Pontotoc Creek. Where Bissell, Mississippi, is today, two major trails crossed. One went southwest toward the Choctaws and the bluffs where Natchez would be, and northeast into central Tennessee. It would be known later as the Natchez Trace. The other went southeast to Mobile, and northwest to the Fourth Chickasaw Bluff. On the northwest leg there were alternate routes to the Mississippi beyond where New Albany stands today. One, the direct way but good only in seasons of dryness, followed the line of Highway 78, eventually reaching the Bluff along the line of Lamar and Marshall Avenues. The other route avoided high water by going due north from New Albany across the highlands to near Bolivar, Tennessee. Here it intersected the main east-west artery across Tennessee, the "Cherokee Trace," on which one turned due west along high ground, approaching the Bluff by way of what is now Jackson Avenue.

In the 18th century the Chickasaws are found living mainly in two long towns, one along the New Albany trail and the other along the Natchez Trace, neither very far from the intersection. They were probably in the same locality in 1541 when Hernando De Soto and his tattered army came among them.

The Spaniards were treated more or less politely till they peremptorily demanded 200 braves as porters. The Chickasaws attacked suddenly and thoroughly: they burned the Spanish camp, destroyed much clothing and equipment, and took away 400 hogs and 59 precious horses. De Soto managed to retreat a short distance and stabilize the situation, and after a period of forging new weapons out of available metal and piecing together skins or other materials as garments, he set out again. After a skirmish at a place called Limamu or Alibamo (a last outpost of the Chickasaws probably where Ingomar, Mississippi, is today), the army plunged into a no-man's land of swamp and forest for eight days. Their exact route, and the exact location of Quiz Quiz where they emerged, has been the subject of much strained theorizing and endless debate, all without much in the way of reliable data.

However, the century-long discussion managed to resolve itself into a choice of three possible sites where De Soto may have first encountered the great river: Sunflower Landing, west of Clarksdale, Mississippi; Commerce Landing, west of Robinsonville, Mississippi; Memphis. The commission appointed by Congress in 1939 to make an intensive study of De Soto's entire route (in preparation for the 400th anniversary of it) gave its preference to Sunflower Landing, largely from reasoning having to do with locations west of the Mississippi after the crossing. But between 1940 and 1947 a survey of all known archæological sites in the lower Mississippi Valley was made under the auspices of the Peabody Museum at Harvard, and it demonstrated the extreme unlikelihood of the Sunflower Landing choice.

De Soto in going toward either of the other two places would have presumably followed the direct Chickasaw trail (Highway 78) to a point near Capleville. Here he might take one of three likely courses, each requiring only a slight shift in bearing. The most southerly shift would take him along the highlands to the vicinity of Commerce Landing. The most northerly angle would bring him to the Bluff in the general area of De Soto Park. A middle course, slightly south along high ground through Whitehaven, would lead to a village known to have been near the present corner of Mitchell and

Weaver Roads. According to De Soto's chroniclers, there were three Quiz Quiz villages in a line, about a league apart, with the last one on the river at a "plain" where rafts were built. The middle village would in this case be Chucalissa on the bluff edge, and the last would have been in Ensley Bottoms.

The question of where the Mississippi was discovered remains an open one. The four basic Spanish accounts are contradictory, and are in any event too vague to identify landmarks, without even considering the changes topography can undergo, especially with the aid of catastrophic earthquakes. There is also the minor point that the Mississippi had already been discovered twice, at its mouth.

Wherever it happened, it certainly bore no resemblance to the mural in the national Capitol, in which De Soto, elegant in plumed hat and fresh satin cloak, surrounded by fashionably dressed followers in gleaming armor, gazes past languorous nude squaws and tepees such as the southeastern Indians did not inhabit. Most of the army was probably more like a certain Don Osorio, described as "wearing a short garment of the blankets of that country, torn on the sides, his flesh showing, no hat, bareheaded, barefooted—without hose or shoes, a buckler on his back, sword without guard . . ." On the other hand, the chief of the Quiz Quiz towns was probably a good deal like Tascaluca, in Alabama, with "headdress like a Moor's which gave him an aspect of authority and a mantle of feathers down to his feet," accompanied by "an Indian of graceful mien holding a parasol."

It was Sunday, May 8, 1541. De Soto called the great stream the River of the Holy Ghost. He would be on the Bluff six weeks building rafts.

Neither history nor archæology has any information to offer about the next 132 years of the Fourth Bluff, except that at Chucalissa a piece of charred wood has been given the radiocarbon date of 1608. At some time during this blank period the Indians of De Soto's time disappeared. No one can say whether it was because of epidemics, intolerable Chickasaws, or other compulsions.

The record begins anew in 1673 when the Jesuit Father Marquette and his fur-trader companion Louis Jolliet stopped at the Bluff long enough to note the anti-mosquito tactics of a people they called the Monsoupeleas or Mosopeleas, who lolled about on elevated wooden grids with smudge fires underneath and a canopy of skins overhead. Their village was called Agenatchi, and they had firearms. On the return trip upriver the two explorers halted at Agenatchi again, and Father Marquette took the occasion to experiment with the mail service. He wrote a letter to whom it might concern, dated August 4, 1673, from the 35th parallel of latitude, and left it with the Indians to see where it might end up. He thought probably the Spanish would get it on the Gulf, but as it happened some Virginia traders came by first and the note came into the hands of Colonel William Byrd (a trader and not the William Byrd of Westover) two and a half years later. The signature reads "Marquet," and has been challenged by those who assert that he always spelled it the more familiar way. The challengers do not say how many other Canadian missionaries of the Jesuit order were at the 35th parallel on the Mississippi on August 4, 1673.

La Salle in 1682 went by the Fourth Bluff without comment, though he left behind a name for the little river there. Supposedly he had with him a Loup Indian called Mayot, and for some reason not too clear the stream became the Rivière à Mayot, or the Rivière du Loup. The former name in time became changed to Margot (Magpie) and the latter translated to Wolf. The Fourth Bluff became Les Écores à Margot for most of the ensuing century. La Salle's 1687 expedition led him to death in Texas at the hands of mutineers, and his faithful followers had to make their difficult way back to the Illinois country along the east bank of the Mississippi. They recalled vividly the hot sands and the stumps and gravel of Wolf River's banks which tortured their bare feet, and the mud where they almost sank out of sight.

The next half-century saw various river travelers touch at the Bluff—French officials, traders, or missionaries, passing by to other destinations and staying at the mouth of Wolf only overnight or long enough to kill the buffalo with which the area abounded. The first visitor to stay longer after De Soto was Jean Baptiste Le Moyne, Sieur de Bienville, governor of Louisiana.

Bienville arrived in 1739 with more than 3500 French and Indians—probably the largest European-controlled army on the continent to that time. His object was to crush the Chickasaws once and for all. These Indians had acquired an undying hatred for the French, who had fanned the flame most recently by a two-pronged attack in 1736. A French force from the north was supposed to assault the Chickasaw towns jointly with an expedition led by Bienville from New Orleans up the Tombigbee. The timing was off, and the Chickasaws trounced each wing separately. Bienville spent the next three years plotting a final solution to the problem.

His original plan was to establish a base of operations at the mouth of the St. Francis, but malaria ravaged his troops there and he moved across the river to the Fourth Bluff. On the heights where the Memphis-Arkansas Bridge spans the river today, "three-fourths of a league" below Wolf River, he built a fort which was finished on August 15, the Feast of the Assumption, and named accordingly. Fort Assumption was of "piles" (upright poles), with three bastions facing inland and two half-bastions overlooking the river. To climb the bluff a zig-zag road was cut, having "seven different and wide slopes" of 140 feet each, with bakeries and ovens scooped out of the earth walls under the slopes. A curious idea seems to have developed that the fort *itself* was a stair-steps affair of seven levels, and the diorama in the Pink Palace Museum is of such a fort. This would be like no other fort known to military history, so far as can be discovered, with no readily perceivable advantage in so novel an arrangement, and several practical problems of defense, field of fire, and so on. The only description of the fort is that of a subaltern who was there, and he says that the river was *reached* by the seven slopes, not that they composed the fort itself. For a 65-70 foot bluff, the seven slopes (perhaps mounting some more gentle swale or ravine) would give an elevation of about ten feet for each 140-foot slant, or a 7 per cent gradient, an acceptable rate of climb especially when most supplies would be carried up by foot, with unlimited manpower for the heavy stuff. There seems to be no reason for not envisioning the fort as a kind of rough pentagon, with the two half bastions guarding the precipice and the other three full bastions looking landward and spaced along the stockade connecting the half bastions, all of it atop the bluff on the flat and open ground.

Inside, the south half was occupied by a battalion of Regulars, while the north half was shared by colonial and Swiss troops. Canadians and Indians camped outside.

The Chickasaws made overtures for peace; Bienville ignored them. But as time went on no one seemed to know whether the enemy were fifty miles away or twice that far, nor did anyone know how to reach them. Swamps and creeks halted exploration, and supplies became a problem. Some Indian allies preferred whooping it up in camp to tracking down deadly Chickasaws in the wintry woods, while more martial types threatened to go home unless the fighting got under way. There was a temporary diversion when three Chickasaws were captured. Bienville reserved the young girl as a slave for the mayor of New Orleans, and turned the old man and old woman over to the Iroquois, who pledged not to kill them. However, the Missouris had made no such pledge, and the Iroquois turned the captives over to them for torture. Such unfortunates were the only Chickasaws conquered by Bienville. Spring floods covered the hinterland, and the campaign had to be abandoned. After seven months on the Bluff Bienville burned the fort behind him, went back to New Orleans, resigned in humiliation, and returned to civilized France.

By 1755 the Bluff was unchallenged Chickasaw country when the exiled Acadians from Nova Scotia drifted by on their way to live with their fellow Frenchmen in New Orleans and in the pages of *Evangeline*. In 1763, foreseeing defeat in the French and Indian War, the king of France turned Louis-iana over to his neutral Spanish relatives to avoid having it fall irretrievably into English hands. A Spanish proclamation put their north boundary on the east bank of the Mississippi at 32 degrees 26 minutes, or at the mouth of the Yazoo. All above this line was acknowledged to be British.

Among the first Englishmen to take advantage of the Spanish withdrawal was Thomas Hutchins, an engineer in the military reconnaissance party sent out in 1766. It is typical of the difference between French and English attitudes toward the Mississippi Valley that Hutchins was the first person since the Monsoupeleas to think of the Fourth Bluff as a place to live permanently. He noted his appreciation of it as "a command-ing, airy, pleasant, and extensive situation for settlements." A later visitor, Colonel John Pope, saw "the most eligible Situation for a Town which I have yet seen of the Banks of the Mississippi." A new era had begun.

For another half century, though, the Bluff belonged to the Chickasaws, who thought it "a pretty place," but saw it primarily as a port to meet supply boats or traders rather than as a dwelling site. The Revolution brought them something of a dilemma: they wished to remain faithful to their old friends the British, but they had also developed many ties with colo-nials, especially James Robertson at Nashville. In 1779 the exigencies of war in the backwoods caused George Rogers Clark to build a fort in Chickasaw territory (near Columbus, Ky.), but he hastily sent Captain Richard Brashears with a supply of goods to the Bluff to stave off Chickasaw wrath. Brashears built a temporary blockhouse to store the goods "at the upper end of this Bluff."

The Chickasaws were wont to resolve their problem by concentrating on the Spanish. James Logan Colbert, the bril-liant Scotsman who had become a chief of the tribe, found Wolf River a handy hiding place from which his flotilla of Chickasaw pirates could pounce on Spanish river traffic. On one occasion in 1782 he seized the wife and son of the Spanish commandant at St. Louis, along with 4500 pesos. He kept his prisoners in a hastily built log jail on Wolf River till they were ransomed. At the end of the war relations with Americans had not been so strained as to prevent the Chickasaws from transferring their old alliance with the British to the Americans, at least where French or Spanish were involved.

The decade following the Revolution was one of increasing American pressure at the Fourth Bluff, with corresponding increase in Spanish alarm. James Robertson reconnoitred the site. The Spanish countered with a Chickasaw treaty in 1784 by which they claimed that nation as a dependency. Putting this claim together with the fact that "conquests" during the Revolution had broken the 1763 boundary with the British, the Madrid government announced its sovereignty over the whole east bank of the Mississippi as far north as the Ohio. American settlers swarmed into the backwoods, most of them angry at the Spanish for closing the mouth of the Mississippi.

In 1787 Spanish scouts reported at least twenty-five American traders on the Fourth Bluff, many of them "vagrants," but including Captain Brashears among them. The State of Georgia sent a party of fourteen to woo the Chickasaws with gifts; unfortunately they were caught by twelve prowling Creeks while building a blockhouse on the Bluff and eight of them were killed. General Wilkinson, meanwhile, published a proclamation urging Marylanders to settle on the Bluff, where land could be had for $100 per 300 acres in perfect assurance that the nearest Indians were over a hundred miles away. The Creeks sent regular scout parties to keep up with Chickasaw plans. The American government wanted a post to divert the river fur trade toward Nashville and away from Spanish Pensacola and Mobile. Chief Piomingo, pro-American and the minority leader of the Chickasaws, wanted lots of ammunition and arms to be used against his enemies the Talapuche Creeks, and the State of North Carolina agreed to send a large supply to the Bluff, including six howitzers. James Robertson and Indian Agent David Henley were appointed to get the job done, and John Overton was their agent to arrange actual delivery in 1794.

The Spanish protested these doings, and Secretary of State Jefferson replied that he knew nothing about them, that in fact he didn't even know where the "Écores Amargas" [Bitter Bluffs] were. The Spanish in Louisiana feared that an American post on the Fourth Bluff would cut off river communication between Natchez and the upper river capital, New Madrid. A Spanish fort, on the other hand, would help discourage American settlement and control the Chickasaws. Accordingly, orders went out from New Orleans to Dom Manuel Gayoso de Lemos, governor of the Natchez District, to erect a stockade at the mouth of Wolf River, first purchasing the ground from the Chickasaws. Judge Benjamin Fooy, highly regarded by the tribe, was enlisted as liaison and interpreter.

In mid-May, 1795, Gayoso arrived at Esperanza (Hopefield) across from the Bluff, in a small flotilla led by his personal flagship, "La Vigilante." Negotiations began for the purchase, but every day for two weeks the Spanish soldiers went over to clear brush on the chosen site. The pro-Spanish majority among the Chickasaws was led by Wolf's Friend (Ugulayacabe, generally known to Americans as "Ugly Cub"), a well-meaning chief who felt he was assuring peace for his people. On May 30 Gayoso felt confident enough to take formal possession. He brought across his artillery (six cannon), ran up the Bourbon banner, and ordered fifteen salvos from his boats, answered by three salvos from the bluff. It was the day of San Fernando, patron saint of the crown prince, and also Gayoso's birthday. The new fort was therefore named San Fernando de las Barrancas, St. Ferdinand of the Bluffs.

In spite of the impressive name, there were no fortifications yet. The first night was spent behind a hasty barricade of felled trees. Next day work got under way and by the time Wolf's Friend agreed on terms, June 20, construction was well along. The enclave purchased was contained by Bayou Gayoso, the Wolf-Mississippi, and Nonconnah Creek. Judge Fooy for

his part in the negotiations was granted 200 acres within the
military area, plus the unique privilege of building a house.
But by tribal law land could not be sold without full tribal
approval, and the pro-American faction, led by Piomingo and
James Colbert's son William, was outraged.

The site chosen for the stockade was the first high ground
south of Bayou Gayoso, in the vicinity of today's Auction
Square. Gayoso's engineer, Perchet, protested the military
folly of the spot: both east and south within 200 yards there
was higher ground from which the enemy could look down
into the stockade despite its twelve-foot height, while the view
upriver was completely blocked by the island at the mouth of
Wolf. General Victor Collot, a French military engineer who
drew a beautifully detailed plan of the fort and its environs,
found the location "inexcusable." Gayoso overruled objections,
however, without giving any cogent reasons. For one thing,
though, he was suspicious of Perchet as a revolutionary because
of a Bastille medallion the engineer had, and, insofar as river
traffic was concerned, a "whirlpool" at the mouth of Wolf
would bring any river craft within "a pistol's shot of shore."

Collot's plan, drawn to careful scale, shows that the central square of the fort was about 200 feet on each side, with
the diagonals extended another 75 feet at the corners by bastions. A force of 131 men garrisoned it, and the commandant
grumbled that three times that many would "rattle around" in
it. Eight 8-pounders served as artillery. Inside the stockade was
the commandant's residence, "a handsome house," along with
"an ill-constructed barrack" for the men and a powder magazine covered with tiles. A 500-foot road ran down the slope
to the bayou, with a rudimentary settlement along it. Eventually
there was a large building with gardens just south of the
stockade, as well as a hospital (with a physician) on the next
high ground southward, and a "habitation" with formal gardens below that. This last was no doubt Judge Fooy's authorized house. A mile south of the stockade, on the slope of a
swale or ravine at about Union Avenue, was the trading post
of that financial empire Panton, Leslie & Co. The warehouse

had been finished in the fall of 1795 by Brashears, who brought six slaves from Mobile for the purpose.

Gayoso regarded the fort as merely an adjunct to his river flotilla, three boats of which were assigned to the permanent defense of the post: the galley "La Felipa," the galiot "La Flecha," and the canonera "El Rayo." These were barges which had been rib-keeled. "La Vigilante" had a galleon type of stern cabin and a huge banner, as well as swivel guns among the oarlocks. These latter were not very useful, but served to amuse the Don as he took potshots at Indians along the banks. At New Madrid in the fall of 1795 he received on board the young Lieutenant William Clark, who came in the name of General Wayne to protest vigorously the new fortification. Gayoso was hospitable.

San Fernando was a hardship post, its small jail usually full of brawling soldiers and sailors, its fevers unrelenting. The food supply problem was finally solved six months after the fort had been destroyed. There was no lime for making mortar, hence no ovens for baking bread. Insubordination was a way of life. Very few of the inmates could have been sad when evacuation and razing was agreed upon in the treaty of San Lorenzo in 1795. Spanish procrastination, however, managed to defer the carrying out of the provision for another seventeen months (in Natchez the treaty was not even made public for a year). On March 6, 1797, the officer in charge of the operation reported that "yesterday we began to destroy the *casas fuertes* of the bastions in order to situate them in . . . Esperanza." Two weeks later men and armaments had been transferred across the river, and the stockade was in ashes. The Fourth Bluff had seen its last European flag.

The Americans had put in an appearance on the Bluff even before the Spanish left. Andrew Ellicott, who had helped survey the city of Washington, was ordered to Natchez to fix the new boundary line. In February, 1797, he touched at the Spanish fort and reported misgivings about the Spanish intention to withdraw. Just downriver he stopped long enough to take sightings to determine where the future south boundary of Tennessee would strike the river. He probably didn't let the Chickasaws see him doing it.

During the four-month interregnum between the withdrawal of the Spanish and the arrival of the American army an English traveler, Francis Baily, drifted ashore at the landing about sunset on May 2. He gives us a rare glimpse of the Chickasaws at their ease.

> These Indians are a well-made, handsome race of men. When we approached the shore, there were a number of them sitting on the banks, and others standing at the top of the hill, enjoying the mildness of the evening and the beauty of the setting sun; others, perhaps attracted by the presence of the boats, whose motions they watched with an attentive eye. However, none of them came to us, or seemed to stir . . . they received us with every mark of friendship and attention. The chief part of them were dressed in printed calico shirts, which (together with what they called a breech clout) formed the whole of their dress, except a pair of mockasons made of deerskins, which are smoked instead of tanned, and are thereby rendered very soft and pliable to the feet. . . . They soon offered us a pipe of peace.

> Soon . . . we observed a boat coming across the river from the fort opposite, and presently Don Grande (who with twelve men commands that place) came on board us, attended by two or three of his soldiers, we supposed for the purpose of inspecting our passports.

Baily had already advised his party to treat insolence with contempt or punishment, but Don Grande just wanted to invite him to dinner at Esperanza, which, Baily noted, was "overflowed . . . or nearly so." The Chickasaws were impatient for the arrival of the Americans, or at least the young warriors were, for they hoped to get military supplies with which to fight the Creeks.

On July 20, 1797, the United States took effective possession. Captain Isaac Guion of the Third Regiment of Infantry and soon to be a leading citizen of the Mississippi Territory, landed at the Bluff with troops he was taking to the new border below Natchez. James Wilkinson, commanding general of the nation's troops with headquarters at Pittsburgh, found him a man of "tried confidence" who had distinguished himself at Quebec in the war. This was not so high a compliment as it might have been, since the rascally Wilkinson had already been in the pay of the Spanish for several years. Guion was ordered to take over all Spanish posts on the east bank, by force if necessary, and to leave gifts at the Bluff for the Chickasaws. Finding San Fernando destroyed, he lingered long enough to build a new "sexangular" stockade on the same spot. By October 22 he could report, "I have this day, having the gates finished and my flagstaff erected, under a federal salute, called the Fort *Adams.*" It proved to be too ambitious a name for the small post.

Why he chose the same undesirable spot as the Spanish is suggested in his remarks to the Secretary of War:

> It seems that Wolf's Friend had sold it to the Spaniards as his land and the others deny his entire right, observing that when the Americans came they should do as they pleased with it. I shall endeavour to obtain the general consent of all the Chiefs and headsmen to suffer us to sit down here; the spot for a fortress is an eligible one, and can, to go below, be abandoned almost any time.

Apparently it was a point of pride with the pro-American Chickasaws that the Americans take over exactly the same site, to show Wolf's Friend who did the tribal buying and selling. Guion was obviously aware of the better possibilities "below" on the high bluffs where Fort Assumption had been, and regarded the new fort as only temporary.

He found four white families in the area who "came two or three years ago and have remained." Only two are identified:

Kenneth Ferguson, the Panton-Leslie agent whose "extortion" had made the Indians long for Americans, and John Mizell (more usually "Measle"), a "harmless" North Carolinian who had lived sixteen years among the Chickasaws. Mizell continued to be interpreter at the Bluff for many years and became a Shelby Countian.

In early November Guion went on his way downriver, leaving Lieutenant Joseph Campbell in charge of two sergeants, two corporals, and 24 privates. Three 6-pounders and two howitzers remained also. However, the following January the commanding general wrote Guion that "Capt. John Pierce has been sent by the Secretary [of War] himself to command at the Bluffs, with a select corps of incomparable rascals under Lewis, Marschaulk, and Steele." Pierce soon died of fever, and Captain Meriwether Lewis was left in command of the two lieutenants, nine non-coms, and 70 privates, until August, 1798, when he was called to act as secretary to his cousin Mr. Jefferson. During the time he was commandant at Fort Adams he was visited by his friend William Clark while the latter was on a river journey. Memphis historians have overlooked this encounter on the Bluff of the young men so soon to be earning imperishable fame.

The Spanish finally gave up Natchez, and a large fort was planned for Loftus Heights near there. The presidential rank of the Adams name was therefore pre-empted for that major post.

The date of the founding of Fort Pickering, the successor to Fort Adams and two miles south of it, has been given as anywhere from 1800 to 1803. The historical marker gives 1801. Yet on November 9, 1798, a trader named William Stanley noted in his journal, "Pass Fort Picering the 9th where git a soldier from Major Pike." General Wilkinson's Order Book is even more specific about the date and the details, and the information it contains is herewith put into the record for the first time.

Wilkinson was ordered to move his headquarters from Pittsburgh to Natchez in the spring of 1798. After a delay at

Fort Massac, he reached the Bluff on August 22, where he found a Lieutenant Marks in charge, whom he ordered to deliver "a description list of the men of Captain Lewis' Company with every paper respecting their accounts clothing &c . . . these men are to be relieved by Capt. Pike's Company."

On August 31 we first hear of the new fort and its name. It is ordered that

> Captain Pike and his Company with a Detachment of Artillerists and Engineers, will constitute the garrison of Fort Pickering on the Mississippi, Lt. Marks is attached to this command and will receive orders from the Captain. The present garrison is to be relieved and will embark with the detachment for Natchez, but this arrangement is not to take place until further orders and in the meantime Capt. Pike will continue to do duty in Camp but will arrange with the Quarter Master and Conductor of Military Stores for the quantum of tools, implements, stores and ammunition necessary to his command . . .

On September 4 the stores, tools, and provisions "destined for Fort Pickering on the Mississippi are to be deposited . . . and the commandant is to be ready to relieve the present garrison . . . tomorrow evening." Captain Zebulon Pike was the father of Zebulon M. Pike the noted explorer, and would remain in command at Fort Pickering till October 22, 1800. He began to build the new fortification two miles south on the obvious high ground commanding a sweeping curve of the river. It was named after the Secretary of State, Timothy Pickering. What had been Fort Adams was now nameless, but still had its uses, and Pike seems to have named it after himself, probably facetiously. It appears as "Pike's Fort" on the navigation chart for several years.

Pike was succeeded in command by Captain Richard Sparks, son-in-law of John Sevier, who was still there in the autumn of 1801 when General Wilkinson came up from Natchez to meet with the Choctaws and Chickasaws at the fort, where a treaty was signed authorizing the widening of the Natchez Trace to a wagon road for the use of white travelers. Governor Claiborne visited in November and Sparks took the opportunity to wangle a transfer to Natchez. Claiborne commended him for his exertions in rescuing several "distressed boats" and much valuable property.

In the Washington administration an experiment had been started in the interests of keeping the Indians happy. Two trading posts had been set up to deal exclusively with the red men, exchanging supplies for skins and furs. In 1802 this "factory" plan was erected into a system by Thomas Jefferson, a benevolent Machiavelli who thought the most merciful way out for the eastern Indians was to inveigle them into debt, take their lands as payment, and offer other land across the Mississippi. Four more factories were set up, one of them at the Bluff, with Thomas Peterkin as factor. He was a salaried employee and forbidden to engage in private trade. He could hire volunteer soldiers at ten cents a day. After a few years the Jeffersonian plan lapsed and the factory was run just as a convenience.

Fort Pickering is known to us more from the descriptions of visitors than from any significant doings of its own. After the Louisiana Purchase in 1803 it was no longer a border post, and dwindled to a mere observation role, keeping check on river traffic and guarding the supplies at the factory. Aaron Burr stopped off at the Bluff long enough to implicate the commandant, Lieutenant Jacob Jackson, in his dark schemes; the forces of the law were in pursuit at the time, and he was arrested a few days after leaving the Bluff. In 1806 the young Thomas Ashe, a touring Englishman, provided the only really panoramic view of the fort. After a glimpse from the river upward where "on the summit of the bluff stands a lonely watch tower, on its brow the garrison and fort mounted with guns," and a rhapsodic view from the heights, Ashe found that in the fort there were

barracks for a company of soldiers and a few artillery
men, and houses and stores for the two state com-

missioners [the factor and his assistant] who reside
there for the purpose of conducting the public trade.
. . . The high plain is very beautiful but . . . is limited
and subsides into ponds and swamps. It maintains
about a dozen families, who raise corn, breed poultry
and pigs, and supply boats.

Ashe was honored with a sumptuous dinner and a "profusion
of wine." He kept to moderation for fear of breaking his neck
scrambling back down the "one hundred and fifty feet of
steep declivity which led to my boat."

Two years later still another Britisher, Fortescue Cuming,
dropped by. He had already visited the Fooys, and on crossing
to the fort he was startled to find the landing occupied by a
painted Chickasaw with bow and arrow in hand. On climbing
the stair of "one hundred and twenty logs" he was further
disturbed to see drops of blood along the way. At the top he
found fifty painted tribesmen hanging around the entry. It
began to seem that he had stumbled on a massacre, to which
he might furnish the epilogue, when he met a nattily dressed
officer and was taken to the commandant, Lieutenant Zachary
Taylor, whose "civility," according to Cuming, "was not
unmixed with a small degree of the pompous stiffness of
office." Taylor would be known as "Old Straight" before he
became "Old Rough and Ready," and anyhow had been
commissioned only a few days.

Taylor had left by the fall of 1809 when a previous commandant at the Bluff returned. Meriwether Lewis was now a
hero and governor of Louisiana Territory. Under attack by
political enemies (cohorts of the infamous Wilkinson) and
emotionally upset, he had set out from St. Louis to go to
Washington via New Orleans and the sea to defend himself.
He developed a fever en route to the Bluff, and then on arrival
he, ordinarily a temperate man, was offered the same alcoholic
reception accorded Ashe. As a result of all these stresses he
went into a delirium, and had to be restrained by the commanding officer, Captain Gilbert C. Russell, to prevent suicide.

After a week under care of the surgeon's mate he regained his senses and seemed normal. He decided to change plans and go to Washington by land. A few days later he plunged into the wilderness and a short time afterward was fatally shot on the Natchez Trace. Whether he died by his own hand or another's remains one of history's puzzles.

While Lewis was at the fort Russell was in correspondence with the War Department about the dilapidated state of the post. He was advised that the season was too far along to commence the rebuilding of the fortifications, but that he should, "with such means as you possess or can readily obtain," repair the "Quarters and Barracks or huts, or build them anew, whichever in the circumstances may appear most advisable." Fort Pickering was only half of Russell's responsibility; he was also in charge of Arkansas Post. Company headquarters and 55 non-coms and privates were at the Bluff that winter. In the spring the War Department grew anxious about the dangers of warm weather in its letters to the administrative headquarters at Natchez. "The post of Chickasaw Bluffs is represented to be unhealthy. What objection can there be to remove, during the summer, the Garrison, leaving a subaltern of discretion with a few men?" This plan was evidently put into effect, as the next fall only one corporal and three privates were reported on hand.

Apparently the garrison never returned in strength, for a few months later the factor, John B. Treat, is found complaining to Washington about the "lawless vending of whiskey and the insolence of the Indians in the absence of a Garrison." It was another year before the Secretary of War even got around to promising a "suitable guard." The fort may already have been decommissioned as a post, since in 1811 the contractor for supplying the river forts was notified that the "Commanding Officer on the Mississippi" has been granted discretion to effect "the discontinuance of any small posts which, in his judgment, might be dispensed with." It would be hard to find one smaller than Pickering.

In December, 1811, John Bradbury, another of those peripatetic Englishmen to whom we owe most of our knowledge about life on the Bluff, was caught in the violent earthquakes which caused Reelfoot Lake while he was on his way downriver. He managed to reach "a log house a little above the Lower Chickasaw Bluff." Most of the inhabitants had fled to the hills, but those remaining said

> that during the shock, about sunrise on the 16th, a chasm had opened up on the sand bar opposite the bluffs below and, on closing again, had thrown the water to the height of a tall tree. They also affirmed that the earth opened in several places back from the river. One of the men . . . attributed it to the comet that had appeared a few months before, which he described as having two horns, over one of which the earth had rolled, and was now lodged between them: that the shocks were occasioned by the attempts made by the earth to surmount the other horn. If this should be accomplished, all would be well, if otherwise, inevitable destruction to the world would follow.

With the advent of war the following year, the regular army had its hands full elsewhere, especially after the successive military disasters in the northwest under Generals Hull and Winchester. The last occasion on which troops were reported at the fort was the overnight visit in early 1813 by Andrew Jackson's abortive expedition to Natchez. His chaplain recorded preaching to about forty soldiers stationed there, who were without shoes and warm clothing in the bitter weather. These were perhaps state militia sent there in the state of emergency existing at the time. No further reference to a military presence occurs, not even a corporal's guard.

With or without protection, the factory remained till at least 1820, and probably till 1822 when the whole system was abolished. It is sometimes confused with the Chickasaw Agency by historians, as on the 1819 town plan of Memphis, or in accounts of the death of James Robertson on September 1,

1814. Robertson died in northeast Mississippi, among the Chickasaws along the Natchez Trace. There exists a supposed "enigma" of history alleging that he died on the Bluff and that news of his death reached Nashville 230 miles away only two days later, when it was published in a newspaper. The only Nashville paper extant, *The Clarion,* published the death on September 8, a week later, and in any event Nashville was reachable along the Natchez Trace in a couple of days, with maximum effort. The Agent was a kind of ambassador, under the military chain of command, and lived with the chiefs. On such rare occasions as the Chickasaw Agency is located, it is at Houlka, Mississippi. There is also the consideration that "Chickasaw Bluff" was the name of high ground near Colbert's Ferry.

Factor Peterkin had been followed in 1807 by Peter Morgan, who was in turn succeeded by David Hogg in 1808. In 1810 Treat took over, lasting till November, 1811, when Robert Bayly was appointed. Bayly died in January, 1814, at a time when there was no assistant on hand. Judge Fooy in Arkansas acted as custodian pro tem, but he hastened to notify the War Department of his concern that more than $11,000 in goods and peltries was across the Mississippi from him and totally without guard.

In May, 1814, the best known of the factors arrived to relieve the judge. Isaac Rawlings had entered the factory service as soon as he reached his majority in 1809, and till now had been assistant factor at Fort Osage (today's Independence, Missouri). He was from Calvert County, Maryland, where he had been born April 12, 1788 to a family of substance: his father was a physician and his grandfather had been a member of the Committee of Safety during the Revolution. He was therefore not a man "of no background" as the historians for some reason prefer to see him, nor was he illiterate. He was highly thought of by his superiors in the service. As a factor, he was on salary and forbidden to engage in private trade. He was never a "sutler" to Jackson's army as has been alleged.

In 1816 Ike was warned not to make any repairs to the buildings beyond the absolutely necessary. A wing of the Cherokee tribe had agreed to move to the Arkansas River, and a new factory for them was being planned there, probably to consist of most of the supplies at the Bluff. In May of the same year another foreign traveler, this time a Frenchman, Édouard de Montulé of Le Mans, visited Judge Fooy. After admiring the Judge's mahogany furniture "of the best taste," his "curious shop full of ancient and modern weapons of every description, which he sells to the Indians," and his generosity in raising ten or twelve children in his own home as though they were his own, Montulé remarked on the abundance of grape vines everywhere. He was told that "a Spaniard living near Chickasaw Bluff" had brought vines from Spain and succeeded in making "some pretty good wine."

The last visitor to furnish a glimpse of Fort Pickering before the Western District was thrown open to settlement seems to be Noah Ludlow, actor and impresario, who saw it in the fall of 1817.

When I first beheld this beautiful site for a city there was not a building, hut, or habitation of any kind on it, — at least where the city is now built; but about two miles below the mouth of Wolf River, near the southern end of the bluff, stood the remains of a blockhouse. This blockhouse was once a portion of the fortifications of Fort Pickering, and had been turned into a kind of trading-store, furnishing shot, powder, whiskey, and other destructives to the Indians, who came here to trade.

At about the same time Ike Rawlings was designated to set up the new operation on the Arkansas, leaving his clerk Paul Ballio in charge of the Bluff trade. Private trading interests had always sought to abolish the factory system, and were about to succeed; in 1822 it would be no more. The Bluff factory would soon cease to be in Indian territory at all, and would become a vestigial affair. Ike began to make arrangements to move in the spring of 1818, simultaneously with the appointment of commissioners to buy West Tennessee from the Chickasaws. Excitement was beginning to grow as land investments made a third of a century before took on the radiance of treasure trove. Within two decades the Chickasaws would be taking up their trek once more, after a half-millennium pause, and this time the magic pole they followed would be the military guidon of the white man.

THE FOUNDING OF MEMPHIS

1818-1820

The Setting

On October 23, 1783, the area that was to become earliest Memphis was tentatively set off from the wilderness all around it. On that day John Rice, a large scale land speculator of Nashville, bought from the state of North Carolina a parcel of 5000 acres fronting on the Mississippi River at the mouth of the Wolf. The fact that it belonged to the Chickasaw Nation by solemn treaty disturbed neither party to the transaction.

Rice was taking part in a huge land grab engineered by his group of land jobbers. North Carolina had agreed to cede to the national government its western territory, the future state of Tennessee, to be held in trust till Indian claims could be extinguished. When it was finally called upon to make the cession at the end of the Revolution, the state government was under the control of the land speculators, and set about postponing the transfer till these profiteers could have their inning. Accordingly, after a large region on the Cumberland had been set aside to satisfy war veterans' claims, in 1783 most of the western territory was thrown open to all comers at ten pounds (nominally $50) per hundred acres. The $2500 Rice paid in a time of financial chaos should probably be regarded as worth about a tenth of that sum for purposes of comparing his price with later ones given for the tract.

A land office was set up at Hillsborough, near Durham, to take entries for wilderness lands which lay some five or six hundred miles away across high mountains. Entries would be accepted beginning October 20, 1783. To claim a parcel of land, the would-be owner first made a rough survey of it, which he then filed with the entry-taker. Thereafter in due time (in Rice's case 1786) an official survey would be made, whereupon the claimant could apply to the governor for a grant (Rice got his in 1789). Such a grant did not become fully effective till entered on the register of the county in which the land lay. Since there were no counties in Chickasaw country, Rice's tract was only penciled in, as it were, so long as the Indians held sway.

Obviously such a cumbersome procedure, for such a long-range investment, would be feasible only for those who had the means and organization to take advantage of it, and beyond the capability of the average dirt farmer. Rice and John Ramsey, whose 5000 acres adjoined Rice's on the south, filed on the same date. Both were no doubt on hand for opening day, but the office was swamped and got several days behind. In May, 1784, those favoring cession took over the state and abruptly closed off the opportunity. It is estimated that something between a half and two-thirds of the available and cultivable land in the western territory was pre-empted by the land jobbers during their seven months of plunder.

In 1791 John Rice was killed by Indians near Clarksville, and three years later his brother Elisha sold the claim to John Overton for only $500, though in much firmer money than that of 1783. Since Andrew Jackson and Overton had a standing agreement about sharing land purchases, Jackson became half-owner of the tract for a consideration listed on the books as $100, a sum not to be taken too literally. In 1797 financial disaster forced Jackson to sell half his portion, a fourth of the whole, to two Winchester brothers, Stephen and Richard, for $625. These brothers, with a symmetry and neatness worthy of a family vaudeville act, promptly turned their purchase over to two other brothers of theirs, William and James, for a quick familial profit at $1000. William died in 1812, leaving his eighth to several heirs, a situation which was worrisome during the planning of Memphis. In a final transaction in December, 1818, after the Chickasaw claim had been abolished, Andrew Jackson sold half his remainder, an eighth of the whole, to James Winchester for an impressive $5000. The acre that had cost Overton 10¢ was now worth $8, even to a business associate.

The new town at its founding, then, had its proprietorship divided as follows: John Overton, a half; James Winchester, a fourth; Andrew Jackson, an eighth; the heirs of William Winchester, an eighth. Eventually James Winchester obtained power of attorney from his brother's heirs, in effect then controlling three-eighths.

Rice began the description of his tract at its southwest corner, given as being on the bluff about one mile below the mouth of Wolf River. In his day the river front was somewhat as it appears today, with a tongue of land separating Mississippi from Wolf in front of the bluff where the town would be laid off. In 1783 the rivers met about where the foot of Jefferson Avenue is today, and the Mississippi's current struck the bluff at what was to become Union Avenue. Rice undoubtedly meant his claim to include some of the desirable high and level ground near today's bridges, and the "JR" he carved on a white oak tree to mark the corner was probably in that locality. Unfortunately, the moody Mississippi gnawed away most of the tongue of land until by 1819 the mouth of Wolf had retreated northward to what is now Auction Avenue. Rice's southwest corner had followed it to a point about where Beale Street now cuts through the bluff. Rice neglected to specify the Mississippi as the west boundary, and this ambiguity, along with that of the south boundary, produced a great deal of litigation in after years.

On today's map the south boundary as it was ultimately fixed proceeds in a straight line eastward from the intersection of Beale and the bluff, picking up the line of Union Avenue at Marshall and going some four miles out to Union and East Parkway. The line of this latter street and Trezevant forms the eastern edge, and the north boundary goes straight back to the Mississippi at about the line of Vollintine Avenue, making an oblong roughly four miles by two. Whatever the uncertainty of the precise bounds in 1818, the undisputed portion of the tract included the most promising site in the whole new territory.

The Cast of Characters

THE CHICKASAWS: The legal owners of West Tennessee and Kentucky preferred to live in what is today the Pontotoc-Tupelo area of northeast Mississippi, on the high ground between the Yazoo and the Tombigbee watersheds, because they found the country along the Mississippi River "leaked too much" to serve as a residence. However, they valued it very highly as prime hunting ground. Its swamps and its fallen timbers left by the great "harricane," its tangled undergrowth and thick canebrakes all gave shelter to an abundance of game. Besides, the Fourth Bluff had for more than a century been recognized as their port of entry and their access to river travel, and they had no wish to be cut off from it. The love of these Indians for their homeland and the fierce valor with which they always defended it had become an epic theme in the history of the red man. In fact, had it not been for their unrelenting hatred for the French and Spanish, and their friendship for the British, the whole country south of the Ohio and east of the Mississippi might never have become Anglo-American at all.

The Chickasaws were ably led by the sons of the late James Logan Colbert, who since his death in 1784 (he was thrown by his horse) had become a legend. William (Chooshe-mataha) was the eldest, and in 1795 had headed the delegation to Washington to protest the building of Fort San Fernando. He led the Chickasaws under Anthony Wayne at the battle of Fallen Timbers, and served in the 3rd Infantry Regiment during the War of 1812. He fought his ancient foe the Creeks under Andrew Jackson, and was awarded a military coat and a life pension for his assistance.

George (Tootemastubbe) ran the important ferry where the Natchez Trace crosses the Tennessee, had 500 horses, and was wealthy in lands and slaves. He was notorious among whites for his arbitrary way of shutting down the ferry at dusk (or sooner if it pleased him), and his extortionate rates. He wore white man's clothes, but otherwise was a reactionary, opposing education, whiskey, and missionaries with vigor.

James, the son of a half-breed mother and apparently without an Indian name, ran a tavern on the Natchez Trace also. He was the best educated of the brothers and usually served as interpreter and correspondent during negotiations. While in a Baltimore theatre in 1816 he had found his pocket picked, and he regarded the United States as a whole responsible for his loss of $1,089. This was fair enough, by Chickasaw standards, for the tribe had always held itself as a whole responsible in case of thievery from white men by any of its people.

Of all the sons, the most revered and influential was Levi, "the Incorruptible," called Itawamba ("Bench") after being awarded a special stool for his leadership in battle. He was elder statesman and decision maker for the whole tribe. "He is to the Chickasaws what soul is to body," reported a white friend. His home was at Buzzard Roost Springs.

Tennesseans considered Levi to be an "artful fellow," but felt that "if Colbert's father the president should humble him a little, he as a good child will submit without a murmur." They also considered it an outrage that "half a dozen Indians, because they are contrary, should be permitted to occupy several millions of acres," and they appealed in the name of "common justice" to the Tennessee delegation in Washington to "do its duty." As a result of this kind of pressure, on May 2, 1818, President Monroe commissioned Andrew Jackson and Isaac Shelby to buy from the Chickasaws all their land north of the 35th parallel and west of the Tennessee river.

The Chickasaws had accumulated much experience in treaty making, most of it disillusioning. In 1786 they had met to define boundaries as a reassurance to the infant settlements on the Cumberland. In 1801 at Fort Pickering (on their bluff) they had agreed to let the Natchez Trace be widened to a wagon road without payment. In 1805 the land squeeze began, and they yielded up all their holdings in middle Tennessee north of the Duck river for a paltry $20,000. Most recently, in 1816, in their first dealings with Jackson as commissioner,

they had lost all middle and eastern Tennessee, as well as substantial parts of Alabama and southeast Mississippi, in return
for ten annual payments of $12,000 each. By 1818 even these
modest payments were in arrears, and the tribe was distrustful
and resentful. Two hundred of them met at Levi Colbert's and
swore unanimously to shoot the first one of them who advocated
meeting with the treaty commissioners this fifth time.

ANDREW JACKSON: By the summer of 1818 the General had
                   become a national hero three times over.
At Horseshoe Bend in 1814 he had crushed the ferocious
Creeks at a time when the more civilized war against the British was going dismally everywhere else. The battle of New
Orleans a year later made him the supreme soldier of the
country (it not being his fault, nor in any way diminishing his
well-deserved fame, that the competition was almost non-
existent in that most wretchedly conducted of all our wars).
In the spring of 1818 he had invaded Spanish Florida and
summarily hanged two British agents there, a performance
which endeared him to the American populace but greatly
embarrassed his government, which was trying to buy the
territory at the time.

In June, 1818, he was recovering from a bad fever picked
up in the southern swamps. He was "reduced to a skelleton,"
and yellow with jaundice, and still had a pain in his lungs and
was spitting up blood. But even half dead he was equal to
taking on the whole stubborn Chickasaw Nation and forcing
it to a treaty council by threat and bribe. He was also deeply
involved in building the first Hermitage, after having lived
on the grounds in a hewn log cabin for years.

Jackson's interest in the Chickasaw Bluffs has been greatly
exaggerated. Newspaper columnist James D. Davis, writing in
the 1870's for entertainment rather than accuracy, goes on
about Jackson's being "anxious to have a quiet retreat," and
that "when Fort Pickering was established" (in 1798) he was
supposed to have bought "a small improvement on the head
of Island 46, where he settled Paddy [Meagher], his wife, and

little daughter Sally." Davis declares that "after the whole territory became known as the Jackson Purchase [i.e., after 1818] and his name was spoken of in connection with the presidency, the name was changed again to President's Island and was perhaps the first compliment of the kind paid to him." All this is blarney, which Davis himself admits was based on yarns swapped for drinks by the deadbeats of the Bell Tavern. As we shall see, Paddy's attitude toward supporting Jackson's claim in the matter of the Rice tract boundary is venal and wish-washy, and hardly consonant with his supposed dependence upon and intimacy with Jackson. Anyhow, Jackson's busy career as a lawyer riding the circuit near Nashville, or as judge of the Superior Court, left him no perceivable leisure to bask in a pastoral idyll with Sally Meagher two hundred miles away in a primal wilderness. Island 46 is called President (not President's) Island by that Bible of Mississippi pilots, *The Navigator*, in the early years of the century when Jackson was still an unknown. It was thought to be (and for a time was) the largest of the islands and therefore "President."

Jackson made occasional trips down the Mississippi, and may well have touched at the Chickasaw Bluffs, but his biographers do not find it worthy of setting down. The one exception is the overnight stop "above Fort Pickering" in February, 1813, when he was en route downriver to Natchez on his ill-fated expedition. Otherwise there is no record until three years *after* the 1818 treaty—and then he stopped off only long enough for a "collation" on his way to be governor of Florida. He has no associations with Memphis except as a paper investment, of the kind he usually left to Overton to take care of. Immediately after the treaty he did not visit the Bluffs, but instead went back to Nashville by way of Alabama where he inspected other holdings. During January-April, 1819, when the town was being laid off, he was in Washington defending his Florida campaign before Congress. On return he was promptly occupied in escorting President Monroe on his leisurely tour from Georgia to Kentucky, and then lamented that he had no funds to travel anywhere. Memphis was very little on his mind at its founding, and the presidency very much so.

He has had about as much experience at treaty making as the Chickasaws. He had negotiated with the shattered Creeks an agreement so ruthless that the government abjured it (partly for political motives), and he had brought the Cherokees to terms along with the Chickasaws in 1816. As general and commissioner, and as president later, he is without rival as the individual American most responsible for the disappearance of the southeastern Indians from their ancient haunts. Davy Crockett was detached enough about Indians to burn some forty warriors in a cabin and then eat, in the cellar below, the potatoes french-fried by the dripping body oils, but he could not stomach Andy Jackson's high-handed way with the red men. Yet it was Jackson who took into his home and reared a little Creek boy after exterminating his kinsmen.

ISAAC SHELBY: First governor of Kentucky, leader with Sevier at King's Mountain, strategist at Cowpens, this venerable statesman was perhaps the most illustrious Kentuckian of his day. A year before accepting appointment as treaty commissioner he had declined the post of Secretary of War because of advanced age. In March, 1818, Congress had voted him a gold medal for his services in the War of 1812. Born December 11, 1750, he too was now ailing and kept in touch with his doctor by mail all through the negotiations. Riding made his leg numb, and he faced without enthusiasm the trip from his home, Traveller's Rest in Kentucky, to the Hermitage and then on to the treaty ground. But it would earn him the right to have Shelby County, Tennessee, named in his honor.

JOHN OVERTON: This eminent jurist, businessman, and politician was Jackson's closest friend and adviser. He was the perfect counterbalance to Jackson's impulsive, often irascible temperament, and Jackson looked to him to take care of their mutual affairs of a paper kind. Sickly and unappealing in looks, he was shrewd and farsighted in business matters. It was he who realized the possibilities of the Rice tract in 1794, and who hung on to his half through thick and thin, eventually becoming one of the wealthiest men in the state. Born April 9, 1766, a year before Jackson, he succeeded his friend as judge of the Superior Court in 1804, and by the time of his retirement from the bench in 1816 he had become a Supreme Court justice and a pioneer of Tennessee jurisprudence. At 52 he was still unmarried, although his home, another Traveller's Rest a few miles southeast of Nashville, was renowned for its hospitality. He was penny-pinching, except in the matter of good cognac, and without much humor or even human warmth of the usual kind, but to him goes the credit for planning the excellent layout of Memphis, for supervising matters carefully during the early years, and for pushing the project at all times till his death in 1833.

JAMES WINCHESTER: A Revolutionary War officer of some gallantry, he moved from Maryland to Sumner County, Tennessee when the conflict ended. When he had become a leader in the Indian fighting, a brigadier of militia, and first Speaker of the Tennessee senate, he built a majestic stone house called Cragfont near Gallatin, married the mother of his children, and legitimized the latter with the flourish of a legislative act. In 1813 he led an army to the River Raisin near Detroit, and to disaster. He and his eldest son, Marcus, were held prisoners near Quebec for many months, but on his return to Tennessee he was greeted as a hero anyhow, and spent most of his time thereafter defending his generalship in the newspapers.

According to his own statement to historian Charles Cassedy, he bestowed the name Memphis on the new town. His landing on the Cumberland near Cragfont was called Cairo, but it is doubtful whether this fact should be held to show his pro-Egyptian leanings in nomenclature. He had originally named the place "Ça Ira!" in honor of the French Revolution, but his backwoods neighbors soon triumphed over the cedilla and other Gallic niceties.

He was always a bit pompous, though congenial enough and generally liked. His troops once reacted to his grandeur by sawing his latrine pole seat almost in two one dark night, with excellent results. He was a staunch republican of the old Roman breed, with sons named Marcus Brutus, Lucilius, and Valerius Publicola—not to mention a Napoleon. General Winchester took an active part in matters relating to the new enterprise on the Bluffs, chiefly those of an operational nature such as supplies, surveying, and the like.

MARCUS WINCHESTER: Born May 28, 1796, at Cragfont, and sent away to school in Baltimore, Marcus left his studies to join his father on the Raisin, where he showed outstanding courage and ability for a lad of 16. He was afterwards called "Major" but was never commissioned nor, indeed, ever enrolled in the army officially on any basis. He was chosen to accompany the commissioners to the treaty ground. Later he will be the one to bear most of the burden of making the town of Memphis a success, under Overton's direction, as agent in residence and one-man chamber of commerce. He will become the first postmaster in 1823, and first mayor after incorporation in 1826. In the 1820's he will marry a kindly and beautiful woman named Mary, who, columnist James Davis says, was a quadroon. Other sources say this was a contemporary misunderstanding, that she was a Creole. This latter word, of course, has one meaning in New Orleans (French-Spanish) and another in the West Indies (mulatto). It is noticeable that no reference to Mary is found anywhere in documents or records of the Winchester family, or elsewhere than in Davis or in the memoirs of her friend Fanny Wright. There is a conspicuous four-year gap in Marcus' otherwise continuous correspondence at about the time when, according to Davis, public sentiment turned against him and an ordinance was proposed forbidding "colored wives" during the period of militant "decency" in the mid-1830's. Marcus married again in 1842, Mary being presumably dead by then, this time to the widow of Archibald McLean, Lucy Lenore née Ferguson, a very young but very faithful and loving wife till Marcus' death in

Upper portion of the 1854 copy of the Archives map. "N. Y. 1827" was added at the time of copying, on unknown evidence. Cossitt-Goodwyn Library, Memphis.

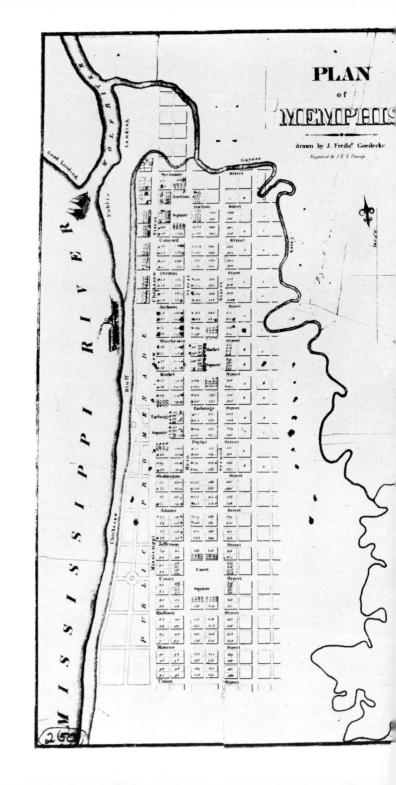

PLAN
of
MEMPHIS

drawn by J. Frede. Goedecke

Engraved by J. E. N. Throop

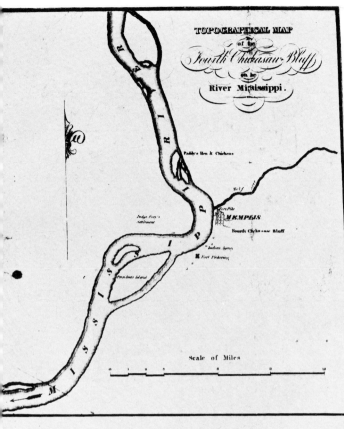

TOPOGRAPHICAL MAP
of the
Fourth Chickasaw Bluff
on the
River Mississippi.

Scale of Miles

Undated town plan of Memphis, in all probability the one drawn in 1819 and engraved in 1820 in Baltimore. Assigned date of 1819 by the Tennessee Archives, 1827 by the Cossitt-Goodwyn Library, Memphis.

1858 copy of the 1829 town plan used to divide unsold lots. Shelby County Register
Plat Book 1.

1856. He was courtly, but never pompous—Mrs. Trollope seems to have found him to be the only gentleman west of the Appalachians. His fellow citizens took him back into favor enough to elect him to the state legislature in 1851.

WILLIAM LAWRENCE: This amiable young man was recognized as a skillful surveyor and generally scientific type. Born March 27, 1798, he will marry in 1821 Eliza Brown, one of the nine sisters of Samuel R. Brown, Memphis' first sheriff and first professional tavern keeper. Lawrence will set up the first "commission house" when cotton begins coming in for shipment, and his home will be the center of the town's early social life. In 1830, the year of his untimely death, he will begin building the first brick residence in town on the southwest corner of Third and Court. He acts as agent for Overton and Jackson, and later for John C. McLemore, while Marcus represents his father and cousins. Some of Lawrence's personal effects, including the goggles he wore while surveying Memphis, are still in the possession of his descendants.

The Curtain Rises
1818

July 7: James Colbert, the most literate of the Chickasaws, notifies Andrew Jackson that the Chickasaw Nation is solidly opposed to a meeting on the subject of selling lands. Jackson, according to his account, "frankly replied that their Father the President . . . only asked them for . . . lands . . . that had been sold many years ago to the citizens of the United States for a valuable consideration, that the citizens of the U. States had been kept out of possession of those lands for thirty odd years that the Indians might enjoy the benefit of the game, by hunting thereon—that now the game is destroyed, and it is of no further use to the Indians, they [*sic*] Individuals who has bought and paid for it demand possession . . . that their Father the President, foreseeing this, wishes as their friend to arrange the business with them by treaty in which will be stipulated to give other lands or a fair consideration in money, that Congress has the right under the Hopewell treaty by law to regulate all the concerns of the Nation."

Just why the Chickasaws should be bound by the sale of their lands by those who didn't own them is not allowed to enter into the justice of the argument, nor is the fact that Jackson himself is one of the impatient "citizens." As for Congress' authority over the Chickasaws, the Hopewell treaty of 1786 did assert the right of "managing all their affairs in such manner as [Congress] shall think proper," but only "for the benefit and comfort of the Indians," a phrase which hardly licenses an act of deprivation. But no matter, both Jackson and the Chickasaws know that history has caught up with the southeastern Indians, and only a show of argument is required, like the courtesy of the highwayman.

August 8:   Colbert relays to Jackson the grudging assent of the tribe to a meeting, but only on their own ground. Furthermore, they will part with lands only "for the price the U. States gets for theirs."

August 11:   Jackson informs Shelby of the Chickasaws' willingness to meet "on the 1st day of October next in the Nation," because his "plain language has brought them to their senses." As for the United States level of price, "these are high-toned sentiments for an Indian and they must be taught to know that they do not possess sovereignty, within the right of domain." He foresees that "we will have to take a high and firm ground," and must counter the resistance of the Colberts by "touching their interest, and feeding their averice." It had long been the policy, and a successful one, to obtain grants and privileges from the tribe as a whole by bribing the individual chiefs. Jackson's word for such an inducement was "douceur." The place appointed is the Old Town of the Chickasaws, within the Nation but at its north border, just off the Natchez Trace, and hence the most convenient location to Nashville.

August 24: Isaac Rawlings leaves the Bluffs after four years residence. He goes with a keelboat of supplies to set up a new Factory on the Arkansas near today's Russellville. He leaves behind his assistant Paul Ballio to take care of the Fort Pickering operation. $11,916 in merchandise, representing part of the overdue Chickasaw annuity, has been shipped down the Mississippi on the flatboat "Good Hope" and wrecked. The salvage is on the Bluffs awaiting disposal. Rawlings will not be back until the new town is more than a year old, and will therefore not be its first merchant as is usually claimed for him.

September 18: Shelby has arrived at the Hermitage and a dinner is given at the Nashville Inn in honor of the two commissioners. One of the toasts given: "While practicing justice to other nations, we should not forget that justice is also due to ourselves." Newspaper observers have "never witnessed an event which has excited so deep, universal, and lively an interest in this state as the treaty." Meanwhile, Jackson has written the Military Agent at Nashville to hold up the rest of the Chickasaw annuity, which was to be paid in cash, until after the treaty council, "believing that great advantage might result" from dealing with non-affluent Indians, and besides such a pressure "will ensure us a full delegation from the Nation."

September 29: The commissioners arrive at the treaty ground. Jackson grouches that they have "found everything wrong, an agent unacquainted with the Indians, the Geography of the country, or even what was the wishes of the Government, and not half the Nation notified of the time or place of meeting—runners have gone to all parts of the Nation to collect them." A postscript notes that "my eyes are weak and my hand trembles—I am still weak and much debilitated."

The commissioners have brought along an honor guard of militia and some interested land speculators. Major William B. Lewis, a good friend of Jackson, is officially commissary officer but is really on hand because he has his eye on a salt spring on the Sandy River near today's Paris. He has arranged to lease it from the Colberts if they can get the area reserved to them as individuals. Another tract, four miles square on the Tennessee river across from Colbert's Ferry, has already been reserved to George Colbert by the 1816 treaty, but only during his occupancy and not for leasing. The government plans to build an armory and foundry in this tract, but another Tennessean, James Jackson, is maneuvering to get in his lease ahead of the government's, if the area can be turned over to the Colberts without restriction. James is not related to Andrew, but has been closely associated with him in confidential business matters.

Soon after the arrival young Marcus Winchester is sent to Fort Pickering to get a report on the damaged goods. Jackson's plan of withholding the annuity funds has backfired: the Indians are incensed at the delay, stubbornly refuse to parley till the annuity is paid, and furthermore insist that it be paid entirely in cash as they will have none of the water-soaked merchandise. Jackson is forced to yield and send to Nashville for the whole $37,550.

October 12: The annuity funds arrive and negotiations get under way. This same day Marcus Winchester returns and gives his inventory of the damaged goods. It was his first visit to the place where he will spend the rest of his life.

In the proceedings which follow, the commissioners have as much trouble with each other as with the Indians. En route they had agreed on going as high as $300,000, though Shelby thought half that should do. Their subsequent quarrel at the treaty ground has two versions. One is that when the offer reached $250,000 without avail, Jackson jumped to $300,000, whereupon Shelby left the table in protest and threatened to go home. They were barely kept from coming to blows.

The other version has it that bidding reached $280,000, payable in 14 annual installments. After a conference the

Chickasaws asked for "one cent more." The commissioners quickly agreed and hands were shaken, but it then developed from the interpreters that "one cent more" was Chickasaw parlance for another $20,000 payment. Jackson assented, but Shelby balked. Finally Major Lewis offered to give bond for the disputed amount in case Congress did not ratify the whole sum. Shelby agreed to this arrangement, but ever after had grave doubts about Jackson's personal involvement in the deal, especially after he signed the bond along with Lewis.

October 19: The treaty is signed: 15 annual payments of $20,000 each in exchange for an estimated 6,469,800 acres (less than five cents per acre), plus James Colbert's $1,089 and other items deemed owing. The salt spring reservation is made to Levi Colbert and James Brown as trustees for the Nation, but they are "bound to lease the said reservation to some citizen or citizens of the United States." The other reservation is made leasable, also, although the United States is given the privilege of taking over both reservations provided it pays the $20,000 to those who have advanced it. This curious arrangement is justified by Jackson to President Monroe: "There were citizens whose interests in obtaining the cession was such as made them willing to advance on the reserve, but we thought it best to hold an election in the Government, and if it choose to make the advance, an assignment will be made on the Deed. . . . We can assure you that without this doceur [*sic*] we could not have obtained the treaty." He later explains to Governor McMinn that he had "created funds out of the property of the Indians, that obtained the cession."

Jackson's political opponents will find this affair a rich lode for their mining, and will attack his business and personal connections with those who profited the most by it, as well as his part in enhancing enormously the value of his Rice tract holdings. Lewis leased the salt spring for 99 years, but the government exercised its right to take over, and there proved to be little profit in the spring anyhow.

October 25: John Overton has been informed of the treaty
                signing. He writes General Winchester that
Marcus has returned to the Bluffs and "is there long before
this. He has fine weather to explore our land there and will
bring us an accurate description of the Bluff tract." He also
urges the General to hurry the clearance from his brother's
heirs. Speed is vital—a town must be laid off "by this time 12
months" in order to beat "the owners of property on the
bluffs of the Mississippi above us."

November 12: Andrew Jackson reaches home after a round-
                 about trip from the treaty ground through
Alabama, where he was allowed to buy land at public auction
for $2 an acre because no one would bid against the hero. He
has not been to the site of Memphis. Shelby has already
returned through Nashville, where a ball was given in his
honor and his portrait "suspended from the head of the assembly
room."

November 24: General Winchester writes Overton of his
                 plans to arrange a "birth" in a flatboat to go
to the Bluffs after the New Year, while Marcus will go overland with the horses. Overton should let him know which
route he chooses (these plans were changed later when the
General was appointed to survey the state line).

The overland route is an arduous one. According to the
Nashville *Gazette,* "persons wishing to explore the Western
District" had three ways of getting to Memphis. All of them
left Nashville by way of Reynoldsburg on the Tennessee river
77 miles away, near the present Highway 70 crossing, where a
ferry took them across to take the "Congress Trace to Natchez."
This is not the familiar Natchez Trace, considerably to the
east, but what had become known as "Glover's Trace" after
the half-breed Chickasaw chief Major William Glover. The
Gazette's name for it comes from the fact that the Western
District had been known since 1806 as the Congressional Reserve.
The trace curved somewhat west, but bent back again mostly
south along the highlands until in the end it brought the

traveler to the Cherokee Trace only 15 miles from the Tennessee river again. One would find "bases of accommodation every 5 to 10 miles" till he reached the new state line (or the *Gazette's* notion of it). Here "Chambers resides, who has 600 head of cattle and sends cheese to the Nashville market." Ten miles further south one turned due west on the Cherokee Trace (which today is some miles north of the state line), being still 110 miles from Memphis, and having still to climb over "the horrid iron hills of Hatchie, and along the levels of Wolf."

On this last long stretch there is no house, but "Tuscomba, a respectable Indian," lives nearby and furnishes passersby with necessities. This is probably the same gipsyish "Tuscombey" whom Governor Blount in Knoxville consigned to Chickasaw Agent James Robertson in 1796 with a note identifying him as "one of the Chickasaws who visited Philadelphia last summer with Col. Hays or Capt. Chisholm, he went last fall out hunting with John Watts, and either in the Wilderness or in Kentucky he met with Captain Lewis who lives at the head of Roanoque and went home with him. He returned to this place yesterday and today I gave him powder and lead, and he sets out for his Nation I suppose by way of Nashville, for I have no interpreter." The distance to Memphis via Tuscomba's is a total of 287 miles from Nashville, and "very little good land is seen on this route," but the pioneer wagons can avoid as many of the swamps and streams as possible.

An alternate route, 33 miles shorter but through more lowlands, leaves Glover's Trace 35 miles out of Reynoldsburg at "Brown's," going westward by way of "Col. Dyer's on North Forked Deer [just northwest of future Jackson] 35 miles, to Harris' Bluff on South Forked Deer 24, to Hatchie 25, to Loosahatchie 35, to Wolf River 20, to Memphis 3." No settlements exist on the last 83 miles. Still a third route diverges at Col. Dyer's and goes even more westwardly by way of Key Corner Bluff and "the mouth of Hatchie." At present on all routes streams must be crossed by "swimming, fording, logs, rafts, and canoes," but ferries and flatboats are promised at major crossings by the spring of 1821.

At some time between the treaty signing and the year's end there arrive on the Bluffs the Carr brothers, Anderson B. and Thomas D., accompanied by their relative and hired man Overton Carr. It has been previously thought that the Carrs arrived in February, 1819, according to James Brown's recollections for the *Old Folks' Record* (I, 404). However, a letter by General Winchester has recently come to light (see entry under date of April 5, 1819) which places the Carrs, or at least Anderson Carr, on the site of Memphis in the fall of 1818. In any event they are the first permanent settlers to arrive after the treaty. They came down the Mississippi, having originally planned to buy land further south below the Indian territory, but on hearing of the treaty when they stopped at the Bluffs, they decide to remain.

December 12:   Andrew Jackson conveys to General Winchester an eighth of the Rice tract for $5000, eighty times its cost to Overton. Winchester now owns a fourth of the tract all told. Marcus has no doubt returned by now with his description of the tract, and this meeting of two of the proprietors suggests that all three were probably present and the layout of the new town discussed. One Memphis legend has the three sitting around a table in the Bell Tavern designing the city, but the fact that the Bell will not be built for several years offers certain problems for this version. The diorama at the Pink Palace Museum showing all three standing on the Bluffs, sketch in hand, is no more historical than the other account. Whether it was December 12, or some other date before Jackson left for Washington on January 7, it must have been at one of the three residences that they planned the city. The Hermitage is central to the other two, and seems perhaps the more likely place.

December 15:   The Nashville *Clarion and Gazette* reprints from the Raleigh, North Carolina, *Register* a biased article which it attributes to General Calvin Jones. The article claims that the Western District is either floodland or "gravelly uplands." On a "narrow strip of bluff" it is conceded

that "Hollanders might possibly contrive to erect a sort of
amphibious town," but that "enthusiasm has made every rock,
swamp and sand hill valuable," with prices averaging $10 per
acre. The Clarion-Gazette indignantly refutes these data. Inun-
dation "takes place but seldom," the soil is not gravelly but
what is called "mulatto land . . . equal to the best," and the
average price is a mere $2 an acre or less.

December (day not given): Overton urges General Winchester to hasten the power of
attorney from his brother's heirs in Baltimore or else set about
petitioning to have the property divided so their portion can be
set aside while laying off of the town proceeds. Winchester in
response arranges for commissioners to be appointed.

1819

January 6: On the eve of Jackson's departure the Proprietors
sign a ten-year agreement providing that the town
lots will be held in common, with proceeds of sales to be dis-
tributed in proportion. They also arrange for various contin-
gencies of ownership should the death of one of them occur.
This agreement will run its due course, and in 1829 the unsold
lots remaining will be apportioned to the individual members.

January 7: The Chickasaw Treaty is officially proclaimed in
Washington. Within a few days the land locating
firm of Joseph B. Porter & Son hear of it and decide to go to
the Bluff. They take along Joseph's nephew, the young James
Brown, who more than a half century later will be one of the
few sources for details of the first year of Memphis.

This same day Andrew Jackson leaves for Washington to
answer charges arising from his Florida hangings, and will not
return for several months.

The new town is one of the best planned of its day. It is
bounded on east and north by the curve of Bayou Gayoso, on
the west by the Wolf and the Mississippi. To the south Union
Avenue will be the limit for surveying purposes, but it is worth

noting that the south boundary of Memphis was never officially fixed by the state till 1832, at which time it was set only as far south as Jefferson Avenue. Four major north-south streets are designed. The one closest to the Mississippi will have buildings on both sides only as far south as Jackson Avenue, and this segment of it is called Chickasaw Street. From Jackson southward no buildings are to be allowed on the river side: all is to be a magnificent public promenade almost a mile long and embracing 14 acres, called Mississippi Row. No cuts are to be made in the bluff south of Market Street. Spaced among the 362 lots are four ample public squares, named by function: Auction, Exchange, Market, and Court.

The Chickasaw "long trail," or Cherokee Trace, coming from the direction of where Raleigh is today, arrives at the Gayoso across from the end of Jackson Avenue, near where St. Joseph's Hospital stands now. Here there is a crossing known as Davis Ford, where in 1825 will be built the only bridge over the bayou for many years. The "short trail," or Pigeon Roost Road, reaches the bayou opposite Adams Avenue, just below a tributary entering from the east. At this confluence later will be Carr's tanyard, and later still the Memphis & Charleston depot. Presumably there is a crossing of the Gayoso here also, but no mention of it seems to occur.

The public landing is planned to be at Auction Avenue, but unfortunately wagons from the east cannot go directly there from Davis Ford because of two deep ravines which reach as far south as the alley north of and parallel to Winchester (in later times promoted to Commerce Street). Wagons, pulled by oxen since the quality of West Tennessee mud made horse power impractical, must turn south after crossing the ford, go down to Winchester and along that street to the bluff, and north on Chickasaw to the landing. This detour causes Winchester to be the chief east-west street of the early town, and it is made 82½ feet wide instead of the 66 feet of other streets, a breadth equalled only by Chickasaw and Main. The detour enhances the value of Market Square, too. A very high hill just west of the bayou and north of Davis Ford dominates the skyline and is not included in the first survey. Also excluded is the low ground to the north between Sycamore Street and the bayou, and that area on the east between the bayou and the alley between Second and Third Streets.

As for the slant-sided area between Union Avenue and the south line of the Rice tract, a newly discovered memorandum by Marcus Winchester sheds some light. It is his testimony in an 1838 lawsuit involving the lots there. The numbers mentioned by him are the lots along the west side of Main Street south of Union, with No. 487 being the southernmost:

The roads which led originally southwardly from Union Street were Indian traces. In the year 1819 one of these crossed Union Street not far from where Main street intersects it and crossing through the land now embraced in lots Nos. 487, 488, 489, 490, and 491, left the strip of land laying between these lots and the river, and which was then enclosed and cultivated and entirely to the west, passing by William Irvine's store . . . on the east side of the trace, and the house afterward occupied by Quimby [?] on the west of the same. This trace passed out of the John Rice Grant near the southwest corner of country lot No. 487 and then inclined to the river.

A little south of Irvine's store and nearly opposite to Quimby's house another trace turned off to the east leading toward Nonconnah Village near Persons Mill.

I do not think there was any trace nearer to the river along the ground for many years, as all the intermediate land was enclosed and cultivated. After the land to the west of them was thrown open and ceased to be occupied . . . then it was that a way came to be opened along Main Street . . .

One of these trails led to old Fort Pickering. The other may have originated in the bridle path which the Spanish commandant of Fort San Fernando had cut through to Nonconnah Creek so he could exercise his horse.

Until 1828 the Mississippi will swirl in under the bluff at the foot of Auction, causing a gentle whirlpool of an eddy which flatboatmen appreciate since they can catch it just right and be wafted north into the sheltered waters of Bayou Gayoso, which accommodatingly broadens out into a placid basin called Catfish Bay. Steamboats, however, find the eddy gives them difficulty in keeping anchored.

There are Carolina parakeets glinting in the sun, and wild swans floating on the clear and sparkling Gayoso as it runs between its grassy banks. The Wolf is so pure that steamboats stop to run its water through their boilers and wash away the Mississippi mud.

January 21:   General Winchester suggests that they try to get a post office for the new town, it being a specially favorable time to do so while Jackson is in Washington to help with the lobbying. Since there is no mail service to Memphis, delivery for the post office would have to "branch off from the Chickasaw Agency" on the Natchez Trace, "until a direct road is opened from one of the post towns on this side Tennessee." Four years will elapse, however, before the first post office is established, though overland mail will arrive regularly from Nashville in only two.

February 2:   Judge Overton publishes a notice in the Clarksville *Chronicle,* which bears also the signature of General Winchester but apparently not with his knowledge. It announces that they or their representative will be on hand at the Chickasaw Bluffs at the house of "Mr. Mahon" (undoubtedly a version of Paddy Meagher's much-abused name) on March 12 next to take testimony about the location of the Rice tract, especially the southwest corner marked by a white oak carved "JR."

February 22:   General Winchester writes Overton that Marcus is all ready to leave by flatboat the last of this month for the Bluffs, down the Cumberland, the Ohio, and the Mississippi. William Lawrence, staying at Overton's, should be alerted and come to Nashville ahead of that date.

February 25: Confusion has arisen. Marcus has seen Overton's notice in the Clarksville paper about taking depositions on March 12. Since it is very unlikely he will get there by that date in a flatboat, he is making a hasty change in plans and will get ready to go overland, picking up Lawrence at Overton's. However, a letter just arrived from the Judge seems to indicate Marcus is mistaken, and the General has told him to "lay upon his oars until next mail" from the Judge. The matter is cleared up shortly and Marcus settles back to await the necessary rise of the Cumberland. Later notices postpone the rendezvous date to May 15 and then to "Saturday and Monday, the 16th and 17th [*sic*] of May." In each ad the assault on Paddy's name is aggravated, with "Mecher" being replaced by "Meaher."

March 7: General Winchester writes William Lawrence, who is apparently staying at Traveller's Rest, to remind him to be ready when the river is. Winchester & Cage will begin loading a flatboat at Cairo on the 9th and will "float for New Orleans with the first rising of the [Cumberland] river and I think you and Marcus must avail yourselves of this opportunity in order to be sure of getting down on time." The General will arrange for provisions and Marcus will take the General's compass along, so all Lawrence has to worry about is his own baggage. He should be in Nashville "by next Sunday or sooner," and leave word at the Nashville Inn so a messenger can be sent for him if he is away when the flatboat arrives, "as it will be unpleasant to have the boat detained more than a few hours."

On this same March 7 James Brown and his surveying party reach the Bluffs. They have just finished surveying, for their own purposes, the south boundary of the state from the Tennessee river westward, and have struck the Mississippi about where General Winchester will arrive later with his official line. Other surveying parties arrive in the next few days: Gideon Pillow (father of the Civil War general), William Bradshaw, John C. McLemore, James Vaulx, and R. Hightower. From Brown's reminiscences, and from other sources, we learn that he found on the Bluffs the following residents who have been "connected with the Indians" for many years as traders and mechanics:

Paul Ballio, acting factor at what is left of Fort Pickering.

William Irvine, living in or near one of the fort block-houses.

Joshua Fletcher, his half-breed wife, and his son Tom. Joshua's father, Peter, is perhaps the oldest resident on the Arkansas shore. Joshua settled on the Bluffs in time for his son Tom to be born there in 1806, and the boy has been "raised in the Nation."

Joab Bean, blacksmith and gunsmith.

Catherine Grace, known as Peggy, living just north of the mouth of Gayoso with a John Grace who may be either hus-band or son. If the former, he has not long to live, as Peggy receives one of the first lots in her own name a couple of months later, and in 1820 will marry Joab Bean.

Henry Fooy, brother of Judge Benjamin Fooy, who is a magistrate in Arkansas. Henry bought an Indian hut some years before, in order to give the "color of a title" in Chickasaw territory. He now has a fine house where Jefferson Avenue reaches the bluff crest today, and a flourishing peach orchard about where Confederate Park is now, with a fenced burying ground nearby. Below the bluff edge, on a batture plain large enough for the Indians to stage horse races, he has a farm with a pond known as Lake Walker (which may be the pond referred to later as being just north of Sycamore Street). At about the time of Memphis' founding he realizes that the river is eating away his farm and manages to sell the land to Paddy Meagher. Just when he left the Bluff does not appear, but it is evidently very soon after selling the batture land, as he does not appear in any subsequent records of the Bluff.

Patrick Meagher, his wife, and his daughter Sally. Before buying Fooy's land Paddy had a woodyard for steamboats on one of the group of islands just above the Bluff which became

known as Paddy's Hen and Chickens. He will try repeatedly
to get a whiskey license, which calls for having a tavern because
grog-shops are illegal. Finally he will make the grade, and a
few years after that will open the Bell Tavern on Chickasaw
Street near Overton.

Besides the Carrs, there is at least one other family not
"connected with the Indians" but come as settlers because of
the treaty: Tillman Bettis, his wife Sally, and their four children. A fifth child will soon arrive, Mary, the first child born
in the Memphis area after the treaty. Tombstones of the Bettis
family burying ground survive today next to a busy supermarket
and shopping center. The Bettises have been on hand "two or
three weeks" when Brown arrives.

Solomon Rozelle, according to his family history, was on
the Bluffs even before the treaty, in the vicinity of where the
Southern Railway crosses Lamar today (Rozelle School is
nearby), and a son, Blackmon, was born there on August 5,
1818. However, Rozelle's obituary in 1856 states that he came
to Shelby County in "1829 or 1830." Supporting this date is
the fact that no contemporary record reflects Solomon's presence
during the early years, and the County Court Minutes include
just about every name in the area as venireman, taxpayer, or
such.

A certain John B. Moore is also mentioned by Marcus
Winchester, but nothing further about him has turned up. His
name completes the available roster of those living on the
Bluff before the city was laid off.

April 2: General Winchester writes Overton: "I hope Mr.
Lawrence and Marcus are at or near the C. Bluffs
by now."

April 3: The exact date of arrival of the two young men who
are to bring the new city into being has not hitherto
been known. However, included in the newly available material
in the Archives is an entry in Marcus' account book as agent for
the proprietors which indicates that the General's hope was

realized. It is an expense account to the proprietorship for "the visit to Chickasaw Bluffs to survey the land and lay off the town." The entry is part of the settlement of General Winchester's estate, and is endorsed "recd this from Maj M B Winchester last of Sep or beginning October 1828 viz 25 Sept ascertained see his acct book p. 294." It is dated April 3, 1819, and in the context of the General's hope would appear to have been itemized during the voyage and totaled up after arriving. Marcus has noted elsewhere that the trip took twenty days, and that steamboats were so scarce they didn't see even one on the whole trip—a fact which didn't keep Judge Overton from advertising "frequent steamboat stops."

The items on the list include "supplies and forage," 150 pounds of bacon, a cable for the boat, a "bed cord for use of boat," a dozen knives and forks, a half dozen each of table spoons, pint cups, and half-pint cups, a tin pan with lid, a coffee boiler, sealing wax and blacking, a curry comb, and a pair of shoe brushes. The total is given as $80.67½, though the items add up only to $41.22.

James Brown remembered that "the town of Memphis was laid off about the month of May, 1819," which is precise enough for a recollection. However, in view of the great haste to get the town laid off it seems reasonable to assume that surveying would begin immediately, and must surely have been under way within a week or so, in early April. William D. "Wappanocca" Ferguson drives the stakes for Lawrence, and Marcus helps as he can. Ferguson will become a substantial citizen of the Arkansas shore, and achieve local fame as employer of Abraham Lincoln.

April 5: General Winchester finds that the depression in prices of tobacco at New Orleans makes it difficult for him to get a room in a boat, but he will go if he has to hire a whole boat, "for I would not for a trifle miss the opportunity of exploring the whole western coast of the state of Tennessee." He sends to Judge Overton for his perusal a letter from Anderson B. Carr, who is at the Bluffs, "now resident at that place, originally from Virginia afterwards of this neighborhood then of Chickasaw County in Kentucky, then of the Arkansas and since some time last fall of the Chickasaw Bluffs."

At some date not long after his arrival Marcus forms a mercantile partnership with Anderson Carr, and it may be that his letter refers to this project. Since the stock arrives after only two months, it would seem that the goods had already been ordered by Marcus before leaving home, and that Carr bought a half interest later. Isaac Rawlings usually is portrayed as being on hand when Winchester showed up, and resenting this young "whippersnapper" invading his mercantile domain. Not only is this obviously a false picture, but there is not that much difference in their ages anyway. Ike is only thirty to Marcus' twenty-three, scarcely the patriarchal image he has been made into, and will not be back in Memphis for at least another year. It seems clear that the firm of Winchester & Carr is the first such establishment in the new town.

April 11:   General Winchester informs Andrew Jackson that he, Winchester, has just been appointed to survey the south boundary line of the new purchase. He hopes to begin by the first of May, and wishes Jackson to recommend a surveyor.

April 13:   Jackson in reply suggests that Winchester get in touch with James Colbert and Colonel Henry Sherburne, the Chickasaw Agent, and meet them at Colbert's Ferry, a few miles from the starting point of the survey.

May ("early"—date not given):   General Winchester comes by river to the Bluffs, bringing his surveyor James Blakemore, to make preliminary observations at the western end of his line before going to the other end to begin the actual surveying. He is using the very fine instruments of General John Coffee, who in 1818 had drawn the south boundary of Tennessee as far westward as the Tennessee river, boundary of the new purchase. Winchester "by experiments" ascertains that Andrew Ellicott was accurate in his observations of 1797 as to where the 35th parallel meets the Mississippi. The General also oversees the town survey being done by Lawrence. The Chickasaws complain later that Winchester was "surveying and laying off a town at the Chickasaw Bluffs before the line was run, and not giving due notice agreeable to the treaty." Winchester, of course, denied that the two surveys had anything to do with each other.

After making his calculations at Memphis, the General goes overland to the Chickasaw Nation where he arranges with the chiefs to meet him on the banks of the Tennessee "the first Monday in June, being the 7th day."

May 22:   If any one day is to be commemorated as the founding date for Memphis, May 22 is probably the best choice. On this day, with the town survey apparently completed, the first lots are conveyed, and temporary certificates of title are issued.

The first lot of all goes, appropriately, to the most influential and affluent man in the region, Judge Benjamin Fooy, still at his estate across the Mississippi in Arkansas. He was the local magistrate under the Spanish regime, and became the American one after the Louisiana Purchase. The proprietors bestow on him lot No. 53, at the southeast corner of Winchester and today's Front Street, "for valuable improvements." This is the approximate location of his house built when the Spanish were on the Bluff, and it may be that some of its buildings were still standing. The house itself is probably not there by now, as it is not mentioned by anyone and was a rather imposing edifice for its time and place.

Lot No. 43, on today's Front Street at the south side of the alley between Concord and Overton, goes to Peggy Grace, and the adjoining lot to the south, No. 44 on the corner of Overton, is given to Sally Meagher. Peggy's lot, after passing through several hands, will be the site of the Bell Tavern eventually.

On this same inaugural day Thomas Carr is granted what is estimated as two acres "on the west side of Main Street extended to Bayou Gayoso and bounded on the north by said Bayou by Mississippi Row extended on the west, and by high land skirted by a pond or swamp on the south, to be designated and laid off by Mr. William Lawrence . . . on condition that the said Thomas D. Carr erect thereon a horse mill for grinding corn for the public, and a blacksmith shop, within one year . . . and a cotton gin within two years . . . and within two years also clean and drain the pond or swamp aforesaid, included within the line of the lot aforesaid." This agreement has not been previously noted by historians, but is among Overton's estate papers in the Tennessee Archives. James Brown's recollection was that in 1820 Anderson Carr received a lot for a horse mill out on Wolf River at Cypress Creek, several miles away, and the other industrial establishments and the swamp have gone unmentioned. Since Tom Carr qualified for the property, as evidenced by his endorsement of transfer some years later, we have a better picture of the origins of industry in the embryo city than formerly.

June 4: William Lawrence reports to Judge Overton, who apparently has not as yet visited the Bluffs. The goods of Winchester & Carr have arrived. Because of this, and because of illness, Marcus has not been able to help with the surveying recently. Since the town survey seems to be finished, Lawrence is probably laying off the "country lots" between the bayou and the eastern boundary of the "town reserve" at what is now Manassas Street, or perhaps those south of Union.

June 7: General Winchester arrives at the west bank of the Tennessee with his surveying party as scheduled, probably bringing the canoe recommended by Jackson for connecting his line with the terminus of Coffee's on the east bank. No Chickasaws appear.

June 12: Facing supply problems, Winchester decides to go ahead without the Indians. When he is six miles along James Colbert finally arrives. He officially approves the survey as made thus far.

June 14:   16 miles under way, the survey operation is joined
               by the other Chickasaw envoy, Chief Sam Seely. He
and Colbert complain that Blakemore does not take his due-
west bearing by the setting sun. The next morning Winchester
asks the chiefs if the rising sun is to be taken as due east (it is
almost at its northern solstice, one might note), and they agree
that it is. The General then aims his instrument in the opposite
direction and points out how far to the south he will now go
into Chickasaw territory. After a hasty conference the Indians
settle for using the compass.

July 8:   In addition to other duties, Marcus Winchester has
              been trying to collect evidence for the original boun-
daries of the Rice tract, and has news for Judge Overton,
relayed in a letter not previously a part of Memphis history.
The "Stewart" mentioned is probably the Captain James
Stewart who is reputed to have acted as unofficial postmaster
in the days before there was a post office:

> Stewart came up ten or twelve days after the
> death of old Mr. Matthews and of his own accord,
> unasked, related to me the dying declarations of the
> old man, whom he says, expressed solicitude at not
> being able to come up personally and depose to what
> he knows concerning Rice's beginning corner. Mr.
> Lawrence being present I requested him to take down
> in writing substantially the amount of Stewart's infor-
> mation . . . Mr. Matthews . . . declared that in his
> opinion the mouth of Wolf River now was greatly
> higher up than when he first knew it—that when he
> first knew it it was nearly opposite to Meghar's house.
> That he thought it now was *three hundred yards* above
> where it then was.

> The old fox Meghar sees which way his wind
> blows, and I think may now be depended upon to
> adhere to the truth. The other day he told me with a
> good deal of apparent warmth and astonishment that
> he saw in Genl. Love's possession before he left him a

written declaration of Fletcher, purporting that in his Fletchers opinion, that the mouth of Wolf had not altered its situation. I do not believe this but if it is so it is well for you to know it.

Judge Overton evidently has been grumbling that Winchester & Carr do not stock enough of the Overton whiskey to suit him. Marcus diplomatically leaves aside the matter of increasing his ordinary stock but will sell "any quantity . . . for the customary commission, and will at all times take from him, delivered here at the river price so much as we may want for our own purposes." But the new store is flourishing: "Our stock is already much thinned—one of us must go eastward soon."

July 13: Andrew Jackson meets President Monroe in Georgia to escort him on a leisurely tour across Tennessee to Kentucky. If one assumes that General Winchester has been keeping his original surveying pace, some three miles a day, he will be ending the state line at the Mississippi about now. He has blazed the trees along the line with a "U.S." fore and aft, and erects a cypress post with the same initials at the Mississippi terminus, somewhere in the vicinity of the south line of Fuller State Park.

The Chickasaws will complain about the line and ask for another survey, but Winchester's line will remain official till 1837, when Tennessee and Mississippi will agree that the 35th parallel is really about four miles further south. More recent surveys give the true position as about half a mile north of the 1837 line, or 3½ miles south of Winchester's, though the boundary has remained as of 1837. There is a tendency to be jocular about the General's inaccuracy, but one should remember that he had one of the better surveyors and the finest equipment available, and that his line agrees with Ellicott's of 1797 and Joseph Porter's of 1819.

July 30: General Winchester is home again. Judge Overton has discovered that the unsurveyed land conditionally given to Tom Carr contains five acres rather than the two it was supposed to have. Winchester resents that Overton would "charge me exclusively with the error. I do not recollect if I wrote the original certificates if I did I know I consulted you concerning it, and that it will be found for two acres." However, when Carr assigns the title several years later, it is for four acres. He gets $300 for it.

In this same letter from Winchester we get a look behind the scenes in the matter of creating Shelby County, including some sidelights not hitherto revealed. William Lawrence has brought the Judge's letter to Winchester, and along with it a specimen petition drawn up by Overton for the erection of a county around the new town. He wishes Winchester to see to it that Memphis citizens sign and submit it to the Legislature. Historians have assumed Overton's part in this project, but have said that his role "could not be stated historically." It can now be so stated.

For some reason the Judge has suggested a triangular shape. The General is puzzled by this novelty, and thinks it unlikely the Legislature would comply. Even if it would, Winchester would much prefer one with four sides "to run East along the [state] Line 30 miles to the 80-mile tree [i.e., 80 miles from the Tennessee River] thence north 25 miles, thence west to the River . . . lay a county in this form you would lose about as much above the mouth of Wolf river as you would gain below the County would be in better form and contain better lands." The General's proposed bounds are those of today, though soon after its inception Shelby County included a larger area and did not shrink to the present limits till 1824. Winchester declares that his "whole and sole aim" in getting the county laid off is to appreciate the value of his lots "by some 15 or 20 per cent." He notes that even Anderson Carr and Marcus "have no other interest than would be common to all the citizens . . . their object is the Indian trade and the Indians care not a cent about Counties and Court-houses. I will however get Mr. L. to copy the petition in the morning and send it to Mr. A. B. Carr."

August 2: General Winchester files his official report on the state line survey with Secretary of War John Calhoun. James Colbert feels entitled to payment as interpreter, and the General supposes $150 or $200 will "not be badly applied in this way." Sam Seely relies on the simple plea that he is a poor man who has had to leave his farm in a busy season.

October 5: The Nashville *Clarion* prints a satire on town promotion methods in the new territory, a mock advertisement for "Skunksburg" signed by "Andrew Aircastle, Theory M. Vision, and L. Moonlight, Jr. & Co."

October 25: The Tennessee Legislature creates surveyor districts for the western region. The Eleventh District will have its headquarters at Memphis, with Jacob Tipton as its Surveyor-General. As a new departure, the territory is to be gridded in five-mile squares by range and section lines, a system which has been working well in the flat states of the Northwest. However, this plan will soon prove unpopular for a country of swamps and hills, and the old colonial system of using landmarks will eventually return. Land offices are set up at Reynoldsburg, Dover, Pulaski, Columbia, and Memphis.

November 24: Overton's petition for a county has been duly signed by Memphians and other settlers in the southwestern corner of the state. On this date the Legislature creates Shelby County by separating it from Hardin County, itself only eleven days old. Shelby thus becomes the first county wholly west of the Tennessee River. Its boundaries are Winchester's. In 1821 it will add areas which will be detached in 1823 and 1824 to form Tipton and Fayette Counties. Its seat is fixed at the Chickasaw Bluffs, but political maneuvering begins almost immediately to locate it somewhere else.

1820

January 11: Marcus Winchester has been to the east coast to re-stock his store as foreseen by him. He has just returned as far as Cragfont and will set out for Memphis in a few days. He takes the occasion to report to Judge Overton on a special mission entrusted to him—the engraving of a map of Memphis which would reflect the survey of lots. This letter is here unearthed for the first time, and leads us into some interesting developments in regard to what has always been a Memphis mystery—whether there ever really *was* a map of the town prior to the one dated 1827, and if so, what happened to it. As a result of Marcus's letter and later ones by the General which also have appeared for the first time, we can say that there *was* a map of the 1819 survey—that is to say, a town plan. Furthermore, Marcus' account of the map is detailed enough to help settle the question.

In the Tennessee Archives there is a map, 20″ x 17″, bearing the engraved title "Plan of Memphis," followed by the legend "drawn by J. Freder. Goedecke: Engraved by J. V. N. Throop." There is no date nor any place of manufacture. The Archives has a notation of the date as 1819, but has no record of the evidence by which this date was established, nor of where the map came from. The Cossitt-Goodwyn Library in Memphis has a copy of this plan, but bearing the date 1827. This date is used because the Library also has a copy of this map made in 1854, at which time after the names of artist and engraver was added "N. Y. 1827." The copy was made by authority of the City Council, to be hung in the mayor's office as reference, according to the Council Minutes. On what basis the added data was accepted does not appear. The copy is only a fragment, without the inset topographical map of the whole Bluff area which appears on the Archives original.

The only other town plan purporting to be earlier than 1827 is the one printed in John M. Keating's *History of Memphis* (I, 144-145), which is identified as "Map of Memphis as Originally Laid Out by William Lawrence, 1819." This map is manifestly not drawn in 1819, since it shows the names of purchasers of "country lots" that were not sold till several years later, and has roads not in existence for a decade or more thereafter. Presumably it is only the nucleus of town lots and the topographical features that are meant. Actually Keating's map is substantially a reduced version of the map used in 1829 by the proprietors when they decided to divide up the unsold lots among themselves. The original of this map has disappeared, but a certified copy made in 1858 is crumbling away in Plat Book No. 1 of the Shelby County Register. A letter from Marcus Winchester in February, 1828, notes that "the staking of the town anew has just been completed by the surveyor." It is obvious that the restaking could not apply to the 122 lots already sold, and indeed may have applied only to the irregular "country lots."

The contours of Bayou Gayoso near its mouth changed between 1827 and 1829, probably because of the high water of 1828 (pictured in the frontispiece) which began an alteration of the entire northern waterfront. Keating's map agrees with the later contours; the Archives map is different. All maps (the undated, the 1827, the 1829, and Keating's) agree as to block and lot sizes, and the widths for streets and alleys. A minor mystery is the name "Water Street" appearing for "Overton Street" on the Keating map, but on no other, nor in any town records otherwise at any time in the city's history. Keating's text gives no clues about his drawing.

We are then left only with the question of the proper date for the Archives map, 1819 or 1827? Marcus' letter of January 11, 1820, describes in perfect detail this map, as he reports to the Judge:

> In pursuance of your directions, that if an engraving of a plan of the town of Memphis did not exceed one hundred dollars, I might contract for the execution of the same, I have engaged a gentleman of the city of Baltimore to perform the same. And I am assured that the whole expences shall not exceed eighty dollars, for which sum I have become jointly responsible with George Winchester of that city.
>
> Having first advised with Mr. G. W., I have caused a topographical chart of Major Long to be embodied in the plate, a steam boat to be moored at

the old Spanish landing, and barge to be represented
under full sail entering the harbor of Wolf river, with
a view to a general communication relative to the
channel of the river, the harbor & landing, which in
your conversations with me you were pleased to
impress on me as points worthy of attention. All this,
which I consider in conformity with your instructions,
will not in the least enlarge the original plan of the
town.

Steamboat, sailing barge, and topographical map are all features of the Archives map (see plate). On the evidence of the
letter, it seems safe to say that the true date should be 1819,
and that the 1854 information is incorrect. If so, the place
should read "Baltimore" as well. The intention of Overton was
to publish the plan in a "popular magazine," but if this was
done, no evidence has survived. It did not accompany the
lengthy account of Memphis in the Philadelphia *Port Folio* of
1820. The matter of Memphis' early maps probably needs further attention; it is reviewed here only as a background for
Marcus' useful letter.

February 24: Judge Overton has proposed to present a Main
               Street lot to his nephew Samuel Overton, and
Andrew Jackson wants to give one to Major James Gadsden,
his aide, which will be charged entirely to him. General
Winchester cheerfully assents to both, and refuses to let
Jackson bear the whole expense.

Sam Overton was described as being "a young man of 25
or 28 years" when he got into a scrape of some kind in New
Orleans in 1817—"not a capital offense," his lawyer assured
the Judge when writing for a character reference. The affair
seems in no way to have diminished the elder Overton's confidence in the young man, as he was named to assume the duties
of the proprietorship in the event of the death of both the
Judge and his agent Lawrence.

James Gadsden was an intimate of Jackson's who had
recently expressed a desire to "abandon military life." He had

also expressed concern that Jackson's career should receive its proper recognition in a history. Jackson therefore recommended him for a revenue post and asked him to write the history. Gadsden deprecated his own ability to do justice as a writer, and explained he only had sought to be allowed to preserve pertinent letters and documents. He later postponed his leaving the service until 1822.

At some time during this year lots are also presented to Jacob Tipton and Major William Bradshaw by the proprietors. The property records do not reflect that these lots were ever actually conveyed. Sam Overton and James Gadsden a few days later received General Winchester's agreement to let them choose a lot anywhere in town rather than necessarily on Main Street, but nothing more about these lots appears on the record either.

March 11: General Winchester highly approves Judge Overton's idea of publishing the Memphis map in "some popular magazine," but thinks the Judge's estimate of "10 or 20 dollars" is too optimistic about the cost. However, Winchester is willing to go as high as $50 if necessary.

April 10: Nephew George in Baltimore notifies General Winchester that the price for the engraving of the map has, in the way of all estimates, gradually climbed as the work proceeded. The engraver is now definite at $96.

April 20: Isaac Rawlings resigns from the Indian service in Arkansas. He has been chafing to get back to his Maryland farm on furlough before the resignation, and probably goes back east before returning to Memphis in the autumn.

May 1: Another commemorable day on the Bluffs. The office of the Eleventh Surveyor's District opens at Memphis for the purpose of organizing Shelby County. On hand for the occasion are Surveyor Tipton and his staff, consisting of Deputy William Lawrence and Clerks John Ralston and William Byler. Land locators remembered by James Brown include (besides his own Polk, Porter & Co.) Memucan Hunt Howard for

Samuel Dickens & Co., O. B. Hays for R. Hightower & Sons, Gideon Pillow for himself, and James Vaulx for McLemore, Vaulx & Caruthers. Judge Overton is also in attendance. The Court of Pleas and Quarter Sessions is constituted by the appointment of five Justices of the Peace. William Irvine is named chairman, assisted by Marcus Winchester, Benjamin Willis, and the Carr brothers. Thomas Taylor is appointed Sheriff pro tem; his term of office proves to be one day.

As a grace note to the occasion Surveyor Tipton performs the first marriage in the new county, that of Overton Carr to Mary Hill.

May 2: The remaining offices of the county are filled: Sheriff Samuel R. Brown, Constables William Bettis and William Dean, Clerk William Lawrence, Register Thomas Taylor, Coroner Gideon Carr, Solicitor John D. Perkins, Ranger Alex Ferguson.

May 3: William Irvine is granted the ferry privilege at Fort Pickering, "at the public warehouse, otherwise called Irvine's landing." Rates are fixed: man and horse, $1; foot passenger, 25¢; four-horse carriage empty, $3, full, $5.

James Swaford posts required bond and is authorized to keep a house of public entertainment, apparently in return for receiving lot No. 24. Paddy Meagher applies for a tavern, too, but cannot furnish bond and is refused license. Prices are fixed for accommodations also: board and lodging, $3.50 weekly; each "diet," 37½¢; whiskey, 25¢ a pint.

June 26: The proprietors of Memphis agree among themselves not to offer lots indiscriminately at public sale, but to sell only to bona fide settlers whom they find to be "prudent and discreet."

July 12: The Nashville *Whig* carries what seems to be the first advertisement about the new town. About the same time the *Portfolio* in Philadelphia publishes an article of several pages extolling the excellences of the infant city in its quarterly issue. Memphis has "some fifty souls," including "several families of the first respectability."

July 28:   The Surveyor-General holds a procession to establish
the bounds of the Rice tract. This same day Judge
Overton is getting married in Knoxville to Mrs. Helen
McConnell White May, daughter of Hugh Lawson White and
widow of Dr. Francis May. This coincidence of events will
prove useful later during litigation about the tract, when opponents of the proprietors will testify that Overton was present
when the tract was recorded, and will be shown by the marriage
record to be resoundingly wrong.

Since the bride has several children, the Judge will immediately set about enlarging the modest bachelor dimensions of
Traveller's Rest. His friend Senator John Williams bets him a
coat he will have an heir within twelve months, and the Judge
accepts, it being a good Overton type of bet since he can't lose
either way.

August 2:   The County Court sets the first tax rate: 18¾
cents per hundred acres for country lots, 37½ cents
each for town lots. The poll tax is 12½ cents white, 25 cents
black. The first year's taxes on the whole Rice Tract: $28.12½.
Six men are appointed to "patrole, etc." through the county for
three months: William Dean, John Riddle, Joab Bean, John
Oadham, John Mazles, and Russell Bean. Mazles is one of the
names for Mizell or Measle, who was on the Bluff when
Captain Guion arrived in 1797.

Russell Bean has a melodramatic history, and an unprom-
ising one for a law officer. He is the son of William Bean, the
first permanent settler in what was to become Tennessee.
Russell was the first "entirely white child" born to permanent
settlers in the territory of future Tennessee. In 1802 he returned
home after an extended absence hunting to find that among
his ten children was a brand new one which couldn't be his.
Wishing to keep the birth records straight, he notched the ears
of the infant. When they came to arrest him he stood off ten
armed men till Judge Andrew Jackson succeeded in facing him
down. Later, while a fugitive from justice, he regained his
place in society by heroism at a great fire.

The first grand jury indictment: Henry Gibson, tippling; case postponed. First guilty verdict and penalty: Patrick Meagher, tippling. $1 and costs.

August 4:   Paddy Meagher finally manages to post bond and gets a licence for a tavern and liquor-by-the-drink. This is not the Bell Tavern as yet.

Tom Carr is authorized $175 for building a "temporary log Court house, Jury room, and Jail on Market Square." It is to be temporary because the permanent spot will be Court Square when the time comes. The new building is to be located on the north side of Winchester Street facing Market Square, at the alley between Main and Second. After the Court removes to Raleigh in 1827 the building will house the first Memphis newspaper. It will also be used all along for church services and public meetings.

August 24:   General Winchester has just received the engraved plan of Memphis from Baltimore, and will send it to Judge Overton "by the first safe conveyance."

Since it is his first communication to Overton as husband, the General offers his congratulations and notes that "You have stolen a march on all your friends in this quarter, to sacrifice at the shrine of Hymen." The amenities over, he goes on to complain about the generous policy of the proprietors in encouraging settlers at Memphis:

> The people of Memphis have taken it into their heads that their settling there is to make the proprietors immensely rich, and that enough cannot be done for them. If we were to give them all lots, they would want us to build for them houses, and next to boil for them their coffee. I am for putting an end to all this, by at once bringing into market at least one half the lots at public sale, say in december next when the land office is opened. Men will easily abandon that which is given to them because it costs them nothing, but make them pay for it and they will cling to it like

grim death to his victim . . . Since personal security
has not been insisted upon by the agents of the proprietors, many of the purchasers of the lots, at least
some of them, are making arrangements . . . saying
they will build a temporary cabbin. If property depre-
ciates in Memphis at the expiration of five years [the
payment period allowed] they can forfeit without
loss, if it appreciates they will hold on and make
money.

September 26: James Brown recalled that Tom Carr was
given two lots in return for building on them
some public accommodations for those who would attend the
opening of the land office. A newly revealed letter from Marcus
Winchester lets us identify the exact location of this enterprise.
Using italics which seem to have some private meaning, he
notifies Judge Overton that *"We have sold Lot No. 146* to
Thomas D. Carr, who has accepted the tavern house contract
and obligated himself to erect the buildings upon the same;
in consideration of which agreed to convey Nos. 45 and 46—
upon completion of same."

Lot No. 146 is on the southwest corner of Main and
Winchester, near the Court House site. Here Carr soon puts up
"six or eight one-story round pole cabins, very low, and floored
with old boat plank, the cracks daubed with clay after the manner of Indian huts." The two lots he receives for his services
are at the southeast corner of Overton and today's Front, and
are not the site of the tavern for which they are payment, as
Brown has it.

Originally some such arrangement was made with James
Swaford in return for Lot 24, but Marcus makes it clear that
the proprietors have been "greatly deceived" by him, and he
has surrendered his title bond and cancelled his notes. Marcus'
final phrase sums up the state of things for almost the next
decade: "No recent sale of lots."

It is probably the added burden of construction that causes
Carr to turn over to Marcus the court house job. It is Marcus,

anyway, who presents to the court a bill for $50 for building court house and jury room. The major items for erecting this economical edifice include $15 for hauling logs, $28 to workmen for "building the house, laying the floor," and $4.71 involved in getting "200 wands used in lining of cracks." Of the original $175 appropriated, $125 now remains for the jail alone. The court officially rescinds the amount as regards Carr and re-appropriates it to Winchester to finish the job.

October 15:   Judge Overton confers with General Winchester about their plans to go to the opening of the land office, announced for 10 a.m. on December 6. William Lawrence has agreed to meet them at Reynoldsburg as guide, and the Judge suggests that the General come and spend the night of November 21 at Traveller's Rest. He should bring a tent and let Overton know what to have ready. The canny Judge notes that he has already had "considerable expense in the pack horse line" and will "propose to find one of my mules gratis—you bring a good pack saddle."

October 21:   Not having heard from Winchester, Overton sends a note by Lewis, his servant, to get an answer first hand. Marcus is to replace Lawrence as guide now, and the travelers should get started on the morning of the 22nd "at furthest." His next remarks indicate that the policy against general public sale has been changed: Does the General know anyone who will make a good "cryer" for the sale of lots? "Much depends on a lively, witty and agreeable cryer," he is aware. But typical Overton caution overtakes him: "Not that I have any idea that it will do in these hard times to give him outstanding wages or hire one at great expense to be paid at all events out of our own pockets."

October 24:   The Postmaster General advertises for contracts to carry the mail from Reynoldsburg to Memphis, beginning December 1, 1820. The rider will leave Reynoldsburg every two weeks at 6 a.m. on Thursday, and reach Memphis, 150 miles away, by 7 p.m. Sunday—barring outlaws, swollen streams, and other diversions. At 6 a.m. Monday he will start the return trip, reaching Reynoldsburg by 7 p.m. Thursday. Similar arrangements are sought for the 130 miles beyond Memphis to "Arkansaw." The contract will run for two years. At last Memphis is on the postal routes, though still without a post office.

November 6: Thomas Taylor is ruled ineligible to be Register because he is already Acting Sheriff of White County. Marcus Winchester, who ran second in the election, claims the job as his thereby, but the court decides that another election is in order, and on the morrow duly elects Winchester. The books have not been properly kept by Taylor, and eventually will be re-done by Winchester.

At about this time Memucan Hunt Howard, land locator, returns to the Bluffs for the land office opening. He stays across the river with Judge Fooy. In old age he remembered the inhabitants of Shelby County in 1820 as including, besides the stores of Winchester & Carr and of "Mr. Rollins," and the Grace, Meagher, Irvine, and Ralston families, "a man named Jones who ran a small tavern at the mouth of Wolf," as well as "a Mr. Robards on President Island," and "a family of bachelors named Person on Nonconnah Creek." Jones may be either the Lewis Jones of the 1820 census, or the Joseph James recently licensed to "keep an ordinary or house of public entertainment at his new dwelling house."

William Person and his brothers Tom, Dick, and Ben are an interesting crew. Huguenots of North Carolina, they have settled on a five-thousand acre tract south of Memphis and built the first grist mill in the county. It is on Nonconnah Creek, "four hundred yards below the Hernando road." William brought the first cotton seed to Shelby County, according to his anonymous biographer. He brought it over the mountains in two or three sacks loaded on "a classic North Carolina go-cart, modeled . . . after the fashion of old Roman chariots." A recluse who "preferred the deep repose and silence of swamps and forests to the busy din and excitement of city life," he dresses in homespun, lives on his own produce, and reads many books in a solitude "rarely broken save by negro servants."

Tom Person is an amateur anthropologist who took a "10-12 year old Indian boy" to live with him just to see if he "could be civilized and raised up on white principles." Unfortunately this red Heathcliffe's "wild nature began to develop itself." The unknown reporter of this experiment concludes: "You may make a white man an Indian, but can never make an Indian a white man—example, Sam Houston!"

December 1: John James Audubon lands for the night at "old Fort Pickering," now in a "decayed situation." He learns that at the mouth of the Wolf, two miles above, there is a landing for "a town called Memphis." He does not go there, though, finding that on the whole the area is rather for the birds. His overnight touching at the Bluffs is enough, however, to earn him a local historical marker—a reward never earned by Marcus Winchester after half a century of service to the town called Memphis.

December 6: The Eleventh Surveyor's District opens its land office for the registration of claims, at the home of Thomas Carr. That ubiquitous citizen has now obtained another lot from Judge Overton "out on Bayou Gayoso for a tanyard site." It is opposite the end of Adams Street at the terminus of the Pigeon Roost Road. Anderson Carr also receives a lot for a horse mill on Wolf River at Cypress Creek.

Judge Overton and General Winchester, presumably with their cryer, are on hand. The Judge is in a good mood, for Senator John Williams is about to win his coat. He has written from Washington to know if the rumor is true that he will win by a margin of two months, and "if Mrs. Overton should except to this enquiry say to her that I will settle the difficulty with her face to face next summer at her own house."

The sale is disappointing, with only a few lots sold, the prices ranging from $30 to $100. But it is more than just good business strategy that impels Judge Overton to reaffirm loudly his faith in the future of Memphis, and more than the glow of impending fatherhood: it is his well-tested foresight and his determination. History has borne him out.

APPENDIX A

FRONTISPIECE: VIEW OF MEMPHIS, 1828

This is the earliest picture of Memphis, appearing here for the first time as far as Memphians are concerned. It is the only one which shows the town when it was still a huddle of log cabins, and is about fifteen years earlier than pictures previously known, which show Memphis of the 1840's, already a line of brick buildings along the bluff. It has been published only once before, in Paris in a very limited French edition in 1904.

The artist was Charles Alexandre Lesueur, well known in his day as a drawer of fauna and flora. In 1815 he was brought over to Philadelphia by the American Philosophical Society, and later made his home at New Harmony, Indiana. From here he made occasional trips up and down the Mississippi River. He sketched not only for science but also for his own interest in the river settlements and their people.

The viewpoint for the drawing seems to be near where Riverside Drive meets Front Street today, just west of City Hall. The two forlorn trees in the middle distance are standing where now the Municipal Auditorium looms at Front and Poplar, and the first rank of log cabins in the background runs along Market Street. The tall building near the river is probably Paddy Meagher's three-storey warehouse.

Besides its great value in revealing a Memphis not previously made visible to us, the picture has further interest because Lesueur happened to arrive at the peak of the record flood of 1828. City Island (or Mud Island, to use the better known name) was not in existence, and the full current of the Mississippi sweeps by the mouth of Wolf River (directly ahead in the trees) in a great swirling eddy only twenty feet below the bluff crest. In normal times a shelf of land extended from Jackson Street north to the mouth of Gayoso Bayou to make a decent landing. Flatboatmen liked the eddy, which could be caught just right and used to propel them up toward the bayou mouth, their favorite landing. Just below this shelf, we are told, a man-of-war could anchor six feet offshore.

The high water of 1828 changed this whole scene by causing the build-up of a batture, or mud deposit. By 1836 a long pier had to be built out over the mud to reach the river. This desertion by the Mississippi had much to do with the southward tendency of the business district in the 1830's.

Our picture is taken from a volume entitled *Les Voyages du Naturaliste Chas. Alex. Lesueur Dans L'Amérique du Nord (1815-1837)*, which reproduced selected sketches from the works of Lesueur in the Museum of Natural History, Le Havre. The volume is in the Library of Congress.

APPENDIX B

THE RESIDENTS OF SHELBY COUNTY AS OF DECEMBER 31, 1820

The 1820 Census:

The United States census taker for Shelby County (a particularly adventurous soul in spelling) in early 1820 listed the heads of families by name, merely numbering the other family members and slaves to a grand total of 364. His list has been made alphabetical below for convenience. The version of the name given in brackets is that which is supported by other records, and identity is presumed.

Alin [Allen], George
Ashford, Butler
Bean, Jocab [Joab]
Bean, Russell
Bettis, James
Bettis, John
Bettis, Tilman
Bettis, William
Bunch, Elijah
Carnes, Joseph
Carr, Anderson B.
Carr, Guidion [Gideon]
Carr, Overton
Carr, Thomas D.
Davice [Davis], William A.
Farmer, George
Fearrell [Ferrell], John
Fleatcher [Fletcher], Joshua
Gibson, Henry

Grace, John
Guibbs [Gibbs], George
Hall, Henry
Harleroad [Harkleroad], Daniel
Irwin [Irvine?], William
Jackson, William
James, Joseph
Jones, Lewis
Maddra (?), William
Maghan [Meagher], Pattrick
McAlester, Robert
McIntyre, John
Montgomery, John F.
Moore, George W.
Moore, Mary
Odem [Oadham], John
Palmer, William W.
Patterson, Drurey

Patterson, Thomas
Person, Thomas H.
Quimby, Robert
Reynolds, Alexander
Reynolds, Nancey
Riddle, John M.
Roberts, Willie

Sawford [Swaford], Jacob T.
Suggs, Robin
Thompson, William
Wade, Enos
West, William
Whitman, Henry H.
Williams, Humphrey

The Minutes of the Shelby County Court:

The names below are not in the 1820 census list, but appear in the Minutes of the Court between May 1, 1820 and December 31, 1820, in contexts which indicate residency in the county (veniremen, appointees, and such). This list is exclusive of the residents otherwise identified in the main text of this book. The three sources together should provide a reasonably complete tally of family names for Shelby County prior to the end of 1820.

Baylis, Paul
Beer, John
Bettis, Drury
Burry, John
Carter, Thomas
Ferguson, Benjamin
Graham, ...
Hardin, William
Holeman, Charles
"Johnaken, Johnathan,
    Johnakin, ..."
Karr, Daniel
Kelley, Arnold

Lamb, ...
Lorance, ...
McGlothlin, Joseph
McGlothlin, William
Manson, ...
Padam, John W.
Pritchett, Richard
Rice, O.
Riddle, William
Terrell, John
Wear, ...
Williams, M.

The Petition of November, 1819:

The 138 signatures which follow are those of persons professing to be residents of southwest Tennessee in 1819 who ardently desire to have a county erected. It was upon this petition that the Legislature created Shelby County; it bears the date of November 4, 1819. Yet only *four* names (J. Tipton,

A. Ferguson, John Moore, and William Erwine-Irwin), or five if the John Burry of the Minutes is also the John Berry of the petition, appear on the other more authentic lists. To take it for granted that signers of petitions are all qualified to do so is politically naive, but one is seldom presented with the impression that virtually the entire population of a county-size region has changed within a few months (between petition date and census). At least 83 different families are named in this curious document. Four signatures are totally illegible, and bring the total to 142. It is transcribed herewith for whatever value it may be found to have.

Alley, Thomas
Armstrong, Lanier
Asher (Askew?), John
Berry, John
Berry, Wm.
Brown, Jno.
Bruce, Wm. C.
Cage, John
Campbell, Arch.
Coal, Loil
Coal, Matthw.
Coffey, James
Coffey, John
Crook, John
David, Jas.
Davidson, D. D.
Davidson, James
Davidson, Mitchell
Davidson, W. M.
Davy, Dunkin
Def................, I.
Denby, Moses
Dewoody, John
Dewoody, William
Dickson, Peter
Dickson, D.

Dickson, R.
Dickson, Wm.
Doheney, G.
Dohenty, Hugh
Downy, Ricd.
Duncan, P.
Erwine, A.
Erwine, William
Esselmon, A.
Esselmon, Alexn.
Esselmon, G.
Fenox, Hugh
Fenox, John
Ferguson, A.
Ferguson, A., Jr.
Findlay, H.
Foster, George
Gale, Wm.
Graves, John
Green, David
Ham, W. B.
Hambleton, James
Harman, John. T.
Harris, Will
Higgins, Bennet
Higgins, Hiram

Higgins, William B.
Higgins, Willie
Hornby, John
Hornby, David
Hugh, Hugh
Jackson, Ln. (?)
Johnson, A. H.
Lawson, Frank
Lawson, Hugh
Leach, William
Leftridge, Ely
Love, J.
Lowry, John (?)
Machin, B. P.
Machin, William
Masles, John
McConnell, J.
McEwin, Peter
McKisick, Wilson
McMillian, Davidson
McMillian, Joseph
McMillian, Peter
Meeks, E.
Meeks, Jas.
Meeks, Jno.
Meeks, Thos.
Mill, James
Miller, George
Mills, Johnathan
Mitchell, Ned
Mooney, P.
Moore, A.

Moore, E.
Moore, John
Morgan, Benjamin
Morgan, Henery
Morgan, Hry.
Moyers, Henry
Moyers, Samuel
Newson, E.
Newson, Peter
Northcut, Peter (?)
Nusom, Daniel
Patten, Edwin
Patten, John
Patten, Tho.
Patten, ...
Porkham, William (?)
Regin, Richard (?)
Robertson, Moses
Scruggs, G. F.
Smith, F. W.
Smith, John
Smith, W.
Taylor, Geo.
Tipton, J.
Van, S. L.
Vance, D.
Vance, R. B.
Vance, Samuel
Wande, P.
Weaver, Jacob
Weaver, Jas.
Weaver, John

Welch, James
Welch, John
Welch, Tho.
Welch, William
White, B. F.
White, Hugh
White, Moses
Whitson, Geo.
Whorton, James
Whorton, Jno.
Whorton, William

Wh............, Frank
Wiley, James
Wilson, C. G.
Wilson, Jno. B.
Wilson, John H.
Wilson, Saml.
Wyatt, James
Wyatt, Thos.
Wyatt, William
Young, Thomas
Young, William

APPENDIX C

SALE OF TOWN LOTS IN MEMPHIS, 1819-1829

On January 6, 1819, the proprietors of Memphis agreed that for ten years all town lots would be held in common, with proceeds of sales divided proportionately. At the expiration of this agreement in 1829 the court was petitioned to divide the remaining unsold lots among the individual members of the proprietorship. 122 lots had been sold when the court complied at its July, 1829 term. The list below is taken from the Shelby County Register of Warranty Deeds, Books *A* and *B*, covering this first decade. It reflects that the property records are about two-thirds complete: 80 whole lots and half portions of 4 others are recorded as conveyed. The list, therefore, should serve as a rough index to the rate of development which Memphis experienced at its start. One notices that until September, 1825, only 3 lots had actually been sold, and these to residents already on hand before 1819. All the others had been given for services or improvements or personal reasons.

Date	Lot No.	Conveyed to:	Consideration	Registry
		1819		
May 22	53	Benjamin Fooy	"Valuable improvements"	A: 200
May 22	43	Catherine Grace	Not given	A: 135;
	44	Sally Meagher	Not given	159; 375
		Unspecified lots were conveyed in 1820 to Samuel Overton, Jacob Tipton, James Gadsden, and William Bradshaw		A: 375
		1820		
Dec. 11	37	William Hardin	Not given	A: 308
		1822		
Dec. 24	52	William Lawrence	"Improvements and services"	A: 305
		1823		
Feb. 6	1	Patrick Meagher	"Valuable improvements"	A: 172
Feb. 6	2	Patrick Meagher	$140	A: 172

		1824		
June 30	49	Marcus B. Winchester	"Improvements and services"	A: 295
June 30	50, 185 186	Anderson B. Carr	$612 total	A: 292
		1825		
Jan. 5	148	John R. Kent	"On condition of building a house within 18 months"	A: 302
Feb. 5	37	James L. Vaughan	Assignee of Hardin (above)	A: 308
Feb. 8	51	James Overton	$1	A: 455
Mar. 2	48	Patrick Meagher	$50	A: 316
Sep. 1	5, 6 44, 142	Thomas D. Carr	In exchange for 45, 46, 145, 146. Carr had received 45 and 46 for building the tavern.	A: 375
Sep. 1	219, 220	Littleton Henderson	"Improvements and $1"	A: 457
Sep. 3	40	Charlotte Ferdam, half	$94	A: 347
		Anderson B. Carr, half	$94	A: 370
Sep. 5	26	Joseph and Thomas Choate	$100	A: 409
		1826		
Jan. 1	150	Jacob Tipton	Not Given	A: 491
Jan. 6	32	Elijah Coffee	$25	A: 407
Feb. 7	183	James Richardson	$40	A: 401
May 30	147	Samuel Rosebrough	$140.50	A: 444
		1827		
Feb. 26	143-4-5-6	Nathaniel Anderson	$4000 for 4 lots	A: 519
June 25	17	Samuel Busby	$60	B: 23
July 4	13	John R. Dougherty	$75	B: 50
Sep. 8	130-1-2	N. B. Atwood	$110 for 3 lots	B: 122
Oct. 2	56	Littleton Henderson	$28	B: 184
Oct. 5	170	Asa Kitchell	$40	B: 14
Oct. 19	155	Zacchaeus Joiner	$50	B: 19
Oct. 19	136, 138	Samuel De Loach	$80 for 2 lots	B: 16
Nov. 16	34	George Aldred	$100	B: 125
		1828		
Jan. 10	187	Abraham Bayles	$100	B: 115
Jan. 25	104	Asa Kitchell	$40	B: 138
Feb. 2	8	Robert Fearn and Robert Lawrence	$50	B: 126
Feb. 2	55	Robert Fearn and Robert Lawrence	$25	B: 128
Feb. 19	57	Samuel Hogan	$100	B: 110
Mar. 3	176	Bazell Bowell and James Walker	$40	B: 109
Apr. ?	195	Nathaniel Anderson	$50	B: 124
Apr. 1	188	Walter Dabney	$125	B: 104
Apr. 7	197, 199	Alexander Erskine	$50 for 2 lots	B: 188

Apr. 12	191-2-3	William B. Dare	$100 for 3 lots	B: 116
Apr. 15	59	Henry E. James	$100	B: 113
May 22	281	Isaac Rawlings	$40	B: 98
May 26	139	Willie Roberts	$75	B: 189
June 4	41	George Aldred	$250	B: 178
July 7	64	Richard Graham	$50	B: 185
Oct. 11	36, 38	George Aldred	Not clear	B: 180
Nov. 8	149	James P. Hardeway	$125	B: 224
Nov. 10	15-16, 21-22	John and Samuel Rankin	$315 for 4 lots	B: 183
Nov. 24	7 (half)	David King	$103	B: 208
Dec. 4	169	Perry G. Nabors	$40	B: 186
Dec. 17	20	John F. Schabell	$75	B: 203

1829

Jan. 1	47 (half), 154	John F. Schabell	$184 for 2 lots	B: 205
Jan. 1	194, 196	Isaac Rawlings	Not given	B: 200
Jan. 1	4	Emanuel Young	$200	B: 385
Jan. 1	9, 10	John Colman	$100 for 2 lots	B: 293
Jan. 1	42 (half)	John R. James	$106	B: 401
Jan. 1	58	"Legal representatives of Geo. F. Graham, decd."	$150	B: 266
Jan. 1	116	Tobias Grider	$75	B: 388
Jan. 1	205	Atwood & Merry	$75	B: 237
Jan. 1	330 (half)	William R. Huntsman	$40	B: 367

The original sale of these lots by the proprietors is not recorded, but they were conveyed as indicated:

No. 180, Winchester & Carr to Amirante Loiselle for $100, November 24, 1827 (B: 100)

No. 17, Jacob Painter to Charles Thomas for $800, March 27, 1828 (B: 120)

No. 74 (half) Walter Dabney to Marcus Winchester, for $75, June 12, 1829 (B: 330).

The 4 lots for which Nathaniel Anderson paid $4000 on February 26, 1827, included as improvements the tavern built by Carr and later added to. Leaving aside this transaction, the proprietors took in a total of $4621.50 in 60 sales. If this total is of the order of two-thirds of the actual sales, the proprietors must have realized something in the neighborhood of $7000 in the first decade.

BIBLIOGRAPHY

The Prologue

Two admirable books by that best of West Tennessee historians, Samuel Cole Williams, include most of the important highlights of the period with which the Prologue deals. They are his *Early Travels in the Tennessee Country* (Johnson City, Tennessee, 1928) and *The Beginnings of West Tennessee* (Johnson City, Tennessee, 1930).

DeSoto

Bourne, Edward Gaylord (editor). *Narratives of the Career of Hernando De Soto.* Trail Maker's Series. 2 vols. New York, 1904.

Final Report of the United States De Soto Expedition Commission. John R. Swanton, editor. 76th Congress, 1st Session, House Document No. 71.

Garcilaso de Vega. *The Florida of the Inca.* transl. John and Jeanette Varner. Austin, Texas, 1951.

Nash, Charles H. "The Human Continuum of Shelby County, Tennessee," *The West Tennessee Historical Society Papers,* XIV (1960), 5-32.

.... and Rodney Gates, Jr., "Chucalissa Indian Town," *The West Tennessee Historical Society Papers,* XXI (1962), 103-121.

Phillips, Philip, James A. Ford, and James B. Griffin. *Archaeological Survey in the Lower Mississippi Alluvial Valley, 1940-1947.* Papers of the Peabody Museum of American Archæology and Ethnology, Harvard University, vol. XXV. Cambridge, 1951.

The Chickasaws

Braden, Guy B. "The Colberts and the Chickasaw Nation," *Tennessee Historical Quarterly*, XVII (1958) 222-249.

Corbitt, D. C. "James Colbert and the Spanish Claims to the East Bank of the Mississippi," *Mississippi Valley Historical Review*, XXIV (March, 1938), 457-482.

Jennings, Jesse. "Chickasaw and Earlier Indian Cultures of Northeast Mississippi," *Journal of Mississippi History*, III, 155-226.

Malone, James H. *The Chickasaw Nation*. Louisville, Kentucky, 1922.

Meyers, William E. *Indian Trails of the Southeast*. Bureau of American Ethnology, Annual Report No. 42, pp. 727-875. Washington, D. C., 1924-1925.

Phelps, Dawson. "The Chickasaws, the English, and the French, 1699-1744," *The West Tennessee Historical Society Papers*, XV (1956), 3-16.

Williams, Samuel Cole. (editor). *Adair's History of the American Indian*. Johnson City, Tennessee, 1930.

Winsor, Justin. *The English and French in North America, 1689-1763*. Vol. V of *A Narrative and Critical History of North America*, ed. Justin Winsor. Boston, 1895.

Marquette and Jolliet

Alvord, Clarence W. "An Unrecognized Father Marquette Letter," *American Historical Review*, XXV (July, 1920), 676-680.

Shea, John Gilmary (editor). *Discovery and Exploration of the Mississippi With the Original Narrative of Marquette et al.* Albany, 1903.

Steck, Francis Borgia. *The Jolliet-Marquette Expedition, 1673*. Vol. VI, The Catholic University of America Studies in American Church History. Quincy, Illinois, 1928.

La Salle

Parkman, Francis. *La Salle and the Discovery of the Great West.*

Tonty, Henri. *An Account of M. de la Salle's Last Expedition.*

.... *Relation of Henry Tonti Concerning the Explorations of La Salle from 1678 to 1683.* Melville Anderson, editor. Chicago, 1898.

Fort Assumption

Claiborne, John Francis Hamtramck. *Mississippi as Province, Territory, and State.* Jackson, Mississippi, 1880.

De Montigny, Dumont. "Louisiane: Histoire de la Louisiane. Poème en quatre chants. Dédié a M. le Garde des Sceaux." Ms. A-4005, Library of Congress.

Harris, John Brice. *From Old Mobile to Fort Assumption.* Nashville, 1959.

Robinson, James Troy. "Fort Assumption: The First Recorded History of White Man's Activity on the Present Site of Memphis," *The West Tennessee Historical Society Papers,* V (1951), 62-78.

Fort San Fernando

Baily, Francis. *Journal of a Tour in Unsettled Parts of North America in 1796 and 1797.* London, 1856.

Collot, Victor. *A Journey in North America.* Transl. J. C. Bay. Florence, 1924.

Holmes, Jack D. L. "The First Laws of Memphis: Instructions for the Commandant of Fort San Fernando de las Barrancas, 1795," *The West Tennessee Historical Society Papers,* XV (1961), 95-104.

.... "Fort Ferdinand of the Bluffs: Life on the Spanish-American Frontier, 1795-1797," *The West Tennessee Historical Society Papers,* XIII (1959), 38-54.

.... *Gayoso: The Life of a Spanish Governor in the Mississippi Valley, 1789-1799.* Baton Rouge, 1965.

.... "Spanish-American Rivalry on the Chickasaw Bluffs, 1780-1795," The *East Tennessee Historical Society's Publication*, XXXIV (1962), 26-57.

.... "Three Early Memphis Commandants: Beauregard, Deville-Degoutin, and Folch," *The West Tennessee Historical Society Papers*, XVIII (1964), 5-38.

Nasatir, Abraham P. *Spanish War Vessels on the Mississippi, 1792-1796.* New Haven, 1968.

Pope, John A. *A Tour Through the Southern and Western Territories of the United States of North America, the Spanish Dominions on the River Mississippi, and the Floridas.* New York, 1888.

Whitaker, Arthur P. *The Mississippi Question, 1795-1803.* New York, 1934.

.... *The Spanish-American Frontier, 1783-1795.* New York, 1927.

Fort Pickering

Ashe, Thomas. *Travels in America, 1806. London,* 1809.

Bedford, John R. "A Tour Down the Cumberland, Ohio, and Mississippi Rivers from Nashville to New Orleans, *Tennessee Historical Magazine*, V (1919), 40-68.

Bradbury, John. *Travels in the Interior of America in the Years 1809, 1810, and 1811,* Vol. V of Reuben G. Thwaites (editor), *Early Western Travels, 1748-1846.* Cleveland, 1904.

Bureau of Indian Affairs, Office of Indian Trade: Record Group 75: Selected Documents Among the Records of the Office of Indian Trade Concerning the Chickasaw Bluffs Factory. Chickasaw Bluffs Factory Records, 1807-1818; Indents Book, 1804-1819; Letters Sent (Books A, B, C, D).

Claiborne, John Francis Hamtramck. *Mississippi as Province, Territory, and State.* Jackson, Mississippi, 1880.

Clark, William. "Notebook, 1798-1838." Ms., University of Missouri Library, Columbia, Missouri.

Cotterill, R. S. "Federal Indian Management in the South, 1789-1825," *Mississippi Valley Historical Review,* XX (1933), 333-352.

Cramer, Zadok. *The Navigator, 1808.* 6th edn. Pittsburgh, 1808.

Cuming, Fortescue. *Sketches of a Tour to the Western Country* [1807-1809]. Vol. IV of Reuben G. Thwaites (editor), *Early Western Travels, 1748-1846.* Cleveland, 1904.

Department of War. Letters Sent, Relating to Military Affairs, 1800-1824.

——————— Letters Sent, Relating to Indian Affairs, 1800-1824.

——————— Letters Sent, Superintendent of Indian Trade, 1807-1823.

——————— Letters Received, Superintendent of Indian Trade, 1806-1824.

——————— Records of the Agent for the War Department in Tennessee, 1800-1815.

Dillon, Richard. *Meriwether Lewis: A Biography.* New York, 1965.

Dyer, Brainerd. *Zachary Taylor.* New York, 1967.

Fisher, Vardis. *Suicide or Murder?* Denver, 1962.

Fry, J. Reese. *Life of General Zachary Taylor.* Philadelphia, 1847.

Lowry, Robert, and William H. McCardle. *A History of Mississippi.* Jackson, 1891.

Ludlow, Noah. *Dramatic Life As I Found It.* St. Louis, 1880.

Montulé, Édouard de. *Travels in America, 1816-1817.* Transl. Edward D. Seeber. Indiana University Publications in the Social Sciences, Series No. 9, 1950.

Phelps, Dawson A. "The Diary of a Chaplain in Andrew Jackson's Army," *Tennessee Historical Quarterly*, XII (1953), 264-322.

Plaisance, Rev. Aloysius, O.S.B., "The Chickasaw Bluffs Factory and Its Removal to The Arkansas River, 1818-1822," *Tennessee Historical Quarterly*, XI (1952), 41-56.

Robertson, Felix. "Death of James Robertson," Draper Collection, Ms. 31-S, pp. 34-54.

Roper, James E. "Isaac Rawlings, Frontier Merchant," *Tennessee Historical Quarterly*, XX (September, 1961), 262-281.

The Territorial Papers of the United States. Vol. V (The Territory of Mississippi, 1798-1817). Compiled by Clarence Edwin Carter. Washington, 1937.

Way, Royal B. "The United States Factory System, 1796-1822," *Mississippi Valley Historical Review*, VI (September, 1919), 220-235.

Wesley, E. B. "The Government Factory System Among the Indians," *Journal of Economics and Business History*, IV (May, 1932), 487-511.

Wilkinson, James. *General James Wilkinson's Order Book, December 31, 1796—March 8, 1808.* National Archives Microfilm Publications, Microcopy No. 654.

————————————— *Memoirs of My Own Times.* 3 vols. (Vol. I: 434-5, 440-458 are relevant to Fort Pickering in this voluminous and rambling work). Philadelphia, 1816.

THE FOUNDING OF MEMPHIS

Books

Abernethy, Thomas P. *From Frontier to Plantation in Tennessee.* Chapel Hill, 1932.

Acklen, Jeanette Tillotson, and others (Ed.). *Tennessee Records: Bible Records and Marriage Bonds.* Nashville, 1933.

Bankhead, Smith P. *Digest of the Charters and Ordinances of the City of Memphis, 1826 to 1860, Inclusive.* Memphis, 1860.

Bassett, John Spencer. *The Correspondence of Andrew Jackson.* Seven volumes. Washington, D. C., 1927.

Cramer, Zadok. *The Navigator: Containing Directions for Navigating the Monongahela, Alleghany, Ohio, and Mississippi Rivers. . . .* Eighth edition. Pittsburgh, 1814.

Davis, James D. *History of Memphis and the Old Times Papers.* Memphis, 1873.

Elmwood Cemetery, Memphis, Tennessee. Memphis, 1874.

Hamy, Jules T. E. *Les Voyages du Naturaliste Ch. Alex. Lesueur dans L'Amérique du Nord (1815-1837). . . .* Paris, 1904.

James, Marquis. *Andrew Jackson: The Border Captain.* New York, 1933.

Kappler, Charles J. *Indian Affairs.* Three volumes (Volume II: "Laws and Treaties" only is employed herein.). Washington, D. C., 1904.

Keating, John M. *History of the City of Memphis and Shelby County.* Two volumes (Map of Memphis: I, 144-145). Syracuse, N. Y., 1888.

Malone, James H. *The Chickasaw Nation.* Louisville, 1922.

Parton, James. *The Life of Andrew Jackson.* New York, 1861.

Peattie, Donald C. (Ed.). *Audubon's America.* Boston, 1940.

Rainey, W. H. & Co. *Memphis City Directory for 1855 and '6.* Memphis, 1855.

Williams, Samuel C. *Beginnings of West Tennessee.* Johnson City, 1930.

———————— *History of the Lost State of Franklin.* New York, 1933.

Periodicals

Anonymous. "The Aborigines of Western Tennessee, North Mississippi and Alabama," *Old Folks' Record*, I, No. 4 (January, 1875), 179-181.

———————— "Mrs. Eliza Lawrence," *Old Folks' Record*, I, No. 7 (April, 1875), 333.

Braden, Guy B. "The Colberts and the Chickasaw Nation," *Tennessee Historical Quarterly*, XVII (1958), 222-249.

Brown, James. "Early Reminiscences of Memphis and West Tennessee," *Old Folks' Record*, I, No. 9 (June, 1875), 403-407.

De Witt, John H. "General James Winchester," *Tennessee Historical Magazine*, I, No. 2 (June, 1915), 79-105; I, No. 3 (September, 1915), 183-205.

Howard, Memucan H. "Recollections of Memucan Hunt Howard," *American Historical Magazine*, VII (1901), 55-68.

Oldschool, Oliver. "Memphis, A New Town on the Mississippi," *The Port Folio* (Dennie's), IX (1820), Article XV, 489-494.

Phelps, Dawson A. "The Diary of a Chaplain in Andrew Jackson's Army," *Tennessee Historical Quarterly*, XII (1953), 264-322.

Roper, James E. "Marcus Winchester and the Early Years of Memphis," *Tennessee Historical Quarterly*, XXI (December, 1962), 326-351.

———————— "Isaac Rawlings, Frontier Merchant," *Tennessee Historical Quarterly*, XX (September, 1961), 262-281.

Underwood, Q. K. "An Address Before the Old Folks, April 2, 1872," *Old Folks' Record*, I, No. 12 (September, 1875), 531-536.

Winchester, George W. "Anniversary Address, August 24, 1871," *Old Folks' Record*, I, No. 4 (January, 1875), 162-171.

Newspapers

Clarksville *Tennessee Weekly Chronicle:* February 3, 1819; March 15 and 29, 1819.

Memphis *Commercial Appeal:* August 10, 1930 (Section V, p. 7); August 14, 1949 (Section IV, p. 5).

Nashville *Clarion and Tennessee State Gazette:* February 17, 1818; August 18, 1818; September 22 and 29, 1818; January 12, 1819; November 30, 1819; July 4, 1820; October 24, 1820.

Nashville *Gazette:* November 18, 1820.

Public Records

Minutes of the Memphis City Council, November 28, 1854.

Minutes of the Shelby County Court, 1820-1824: pp. 1, 11, 17-21, 26-30, 49-51.

Shelby County Marriage Records, 1819-1850, compiled by the Memphis Genealogical Society, 1957: p. 10, 23.

Shelby County Probate Court Minutes Book, No. 2 (1824-29), Part 1, p. 39, 62.

Shelby County Register of Warranty Deeds: Book *A,* 92, 135, 149, 159, 200, 375; Book *B,* 218.

Shelby County Register, Plat Book No. 1 (The copy of the 1829 Memphis map is tucked between the final page and the cover.)

Manuscripts

Claybrooke-Overton Collection. Tennessee Archives.
    Container No. 8: Folders 6, 11, 14.
    Container No. 11: Folders 1, 2, 6.
    Container No. 13: Folder 18.

Goedecke, J. Frederick. *Plan of Memphis.* Tennessee Archives. Engraved by J. V. N. Throop, no date.

Goedecke, J. Frederick. *Plan of Memphis.* Cossitt-Goodwyn Library, Memphis. Republished by W. Crane, City Civil Engineer, in 1854, with added legend "N. Y., 1827."

Jones Family Papers. Tennessee Archives. Container No. 9: Folder 14.

John Overton Papers. Joint Universities' Library, Nashville, Tennessee. John M. Lea, "Sketch of John Overton."

James Robertson Papers. Tennessee Archives. Container No. 1; Folder 13.

Rozelle Family History. Y. Rozelle Holman, Memphis, Tennessee.

Shelby Family Papers. Volume 5 (1817-1819). Library of Congress.

James Winchester Papers. Tennessee Archives. Container No. 2: Folders 1 and 3.